ECONOMIC THEORY

ECONOMIC THEORY
A Critic's Companion

M.A.G. van Meerhaeghe
State University of Ghent

Martinus Nijhoff Publishing
Boston/The Hague/London

Distributors:
Martinus Nijhoff Publishing
Kluwer Boston, Inc.
160 Old Derby Street
Hingham, Massachusetts 02043

Library of Congress Cataloging in Publication Data

Meerhaeghe, Marcel Alfons Gilbert van, 1921–
Economic theory.

Includes bibliographical references and index.
1. Economics. I. Title.
HB171.5.M5112 330 79-22215
ISBN 0-89838-027-8

Printed in the United States of America.

PREFACE

In preparing the eighth edition of my *Handboek van de Economie* (an earlier edition has been translated into English, *Economics a critical approach*), the contents have been divided into two parts. Whereas the first part deals with economic theory as such, the present publication contains the subject matter of the second part, namely, the critical comments on various economic theories. Here I have taken into consideration the opinions expressed in reviews of the aforementioned book and by several colleagues. While some indicated that 'The "appraisal" sections cater for the sceptical intelligent student' (C.D. Harbury, *Economica,* August 1972), other teachers judge that 'students who demand "relevance" from their studies are not likely to last long with a book which follows each point by a note stating that it is really pretty useless' (J.R.S. Revell, *The Economic Journal,* September 1972).

This book has no intentions of instructing fellow economists. It is intended as a complement to an introductory course on economics, which for the most part does not deal systematically with (or is even totally lacking in) critical comments. This also explains why a survey of the main trends in economic doctrine are found in the Appendix.

Many economists consider any criticism of economic theory to be a form of *lesè-majesté*. On the other hand, a critical approach should not be the monopoly of Marxist or gauchist authors.

My thanks are due to Prof. P. Hennipman, who was kind enough to read and comment on the manuscript, but who, although I took his remarks into consideration as far as possible, shares the opinion expressed by Prof. Revell. Acknowledgments also to Mr. John Cairns, FIL, for handling the linguistic aspect of the manuscript.

I am indebted to my assistants, and especially Mr. H. Baert, for their cooperation in the production of this book. Mr. Baert also undertook to compile the indexes and to check many bibliographical details.

My thanks are also due to my wife who gave useful assistance at every stage of the project.

CONTENTS

Preface v

1 **Introduction** 1
  1. Terminology 2
  2. Originality 4
  3. Ideology 4

2 **The theory of the consumer's behaviour** 9
  1. Gossen's 'laws' 9
  2. The indifference curves 10
  3. The influence of the other consumers 12
  4. Demand 13
  5. Consumption and saving 14
  6. Conclusion 15

3 **The theory of producer's behaviour** 17
  1. Substitutability and complementarity of production factors 17
  2. The optimum combination of factors for a given level of output 18

3. Optimum level of production 19
4. Supply and revenue 20
5. The investment decision 21
6. Conclusion 22

4 The theory of pricing 23
1. Marginalism 23
2. Corporate objectives 25
3. Instruments of corporate policy 26
a. Price 27
b. Quality 27
c. Sales promotion 28
d. Distribution 28
e. Product range 29
4. Price interdependence 29
5. The 'laws' of supply and demand 29
6. Conclusion 30

5 The theory of income distribution 33
1. The labour market 34
a. Unions and the wage level 35
b. Wage differentials 37
2. The market for loanable funds 38
3. Conclusion 41

6 The theory of the general level of national income and of prices 43
1. Monetary equilibrium and the level of national income 43
a. The investment multiplier 44
b. The accelerator 45
c. The interaction 46
2. Inflation 46
3. The transactions equation and the quantity theory 47
a. The transactions equation of exchange 47
b. The quantity theory 48
4. The cash-balance theory 49
5. Conclusion 50

7 The theory of economic growth 51
1. The Harrod-Domar theory 52
2. The neoclassical theory 53

3. W. Rostow's theory 53
4. The factors of economic growth 54
   a. Population 54
   b. Natural conditions 54
   c. Capital 55
   d. Education 55
   e. Technological advance 56
5. Conclusion 57

8 The theory of international trade 59
1. The theory of comparative cost 59
2. The Heckscher-Ohlin theory 61
3. Trade and economic growth 62
4. The theory of purchasing-power parity 64
5. The theory of balance-of-payments equilibrium 65
6. Conclusion 66

9 The limited practicability of the theory 69
1. Isolation from other sciences 69
2. Unrealistic hypotheses 71
   a. Testing and falsifying 71
   b. Nonoperational concepts 72
3. Mathematization of economics 72
4. Conclusion 75

10 The significance of economic theory 77
1. Determinism 77
2. Predictability 77
3. Theory or method? 80
4. Conclusion 81

Appendix Economic Doctrines 83
1. Ancient and Medieval times 83
2. Mercantilism 84
3. Physiocracy 87
4. The classical school 89
5. The historical school 92
6. Socialism 93
7. The Austrian school and the Lausanne school 99
8. Neoclassicism and the Swedish school 101

9. Institutionalism 102
10. The Keynesian 'revolution' 104
11. J.A. Schumpeter 105
12. Neo-Marxism 106
13. Neoliberalism 107

Endnotes 111
Index 125

1 INTRODUCTION

Economic science has always been the subject of criticism, especially during the depression of the thirties and after the Second World War, when I, among others, deplored that: '. . . so much energy was wasted in obtaining so few results, or in discussing matters of practically no importance.'[(1)]

In 1958, P. Hennipman stated: 'For some time now, more and more symptoms of serious discontent and concern about the present state and recent development of economic science have been observed.'[(2)] This sentence, with which he opened a thorough and erudite essay on 'Recent criticism of economic science', applies with even greater force in the present situation. Numerous books and articles are still being devoted to the crisis. Among the most recent are the not very systematic publications of J. Robinson[(3)] and the less original works of A. Lowe[(4)] and B. Ward.[(5)] In our view, *the* most eminent work remains that by S. Schoeffler.[(6)]

Before embarking in the following chapters upon a critique of economic science, I shall expand upon terminological confusion and plagiarism, ailments that afflict economics as well as other social sciences. Finally, attention shall be drawn to the relationship between ideology and economics.

1. TERMINOLOGY

Unfortunately, in economics the simplest concepts are defined in numerous and divergent ways. For example, one need only point to the number of different meanings of *capital* and *capitalism;* the same applies to economic structure (some authors consider technological knowledge as a structural element, others do not), national product, national wealth; and finally, endless terminological disputes have arisen from the link between *saving* and *investment.*

My complaint is by no means original. In the last century, Malthus spoke of the defective formulation of concepts in economics,[(7)] and in 1937 R. Miry wrote:

> . . . it would be hard to dream up a bigger muddle than the terminology we employ. In many cases we do not even understand each other because we assign the most varied meanings to one and the same word. We are living in a tower of Babel . . . continuously aggravated by acrobatic terms which we forge in order to look more learned than a colleague or to have the air of saying something different from a predecessor.[(8)]

Ten years later, J.S. Davis was warning us:

> If economics is to deserve recognition as a science, even in the modest sense of orderly arrangement of better knowledge, we need to do better in choosing and clarifying elementary concepts, standardizing terms, and becoming more explicit and consistent in our use of both,[(9)]

and C.F. Carter joins him when he speaks of economics as an 'immensely complex subject, with no agreed notation or set of definitions.'[(10)]

There is not even unanimity concerning the definitions of economics. Some authors simply put forward the view that 'Economics is what economists do' (K.E. Boulding), or 'Economics is the study of economics' (D. Seers). The controversy between the champions of the various definitions, according to W. Eucken a 'nutzloser Streit', has, in any case, brought few results.(11)

Apparently, economic associations find it beneath their dignity to devote a congress to the matter. Even if such a gathering confined itself to bringing a certain degree of uniformity in mathematical symbols, it would have performed a useful service.

And even when there is a certain agreement on a concept, economists often lose sight of the fact that interpretation of the concept is difficult. This can be illustrated by the following examples.

International comparisons of statistics on the national product must be made with caution, not only due to the divergent relative importance of incomes of, for example, members of the armed forces and intermediaries in the distribution process, but also because the accuracy with which the national product is calculated varies considerably from country to country (and exchange rates do not accord with purchasing power parities). In most of the less-developed countries a good deal of juggling has been needed to draw up national income statistics. The less-developed countries are not as poor as the figures indicate. In those countries untraded goods are cheaper than in the developed countries. A comparison between the real income of Thailand and that of the United Kingdom has shown that the former figure is 470 percent higher than the amount that would be obtained by converting the money income of both countries into a common currency.(12)

Partial productivity (the ratio of output to a single factor, e.g. labour, both expressed in money terms) as a yardstick of economic efficiency is significant only if there has been no factor substitution (or change in the factor combination). Even then, it is doubtful whether the value of the different types of labour (which, moreover, do not remain unchanged) can be added up.

F. Schaller correctly observes that in the literature we can find the most varied formulas for measuring productivity, but that the real difficulty is to establish what productivity is, what the object of our research is, and what precise significance we ought to attribute to the information found.(13) One therefore wonders whether it would not be preferable to substitute the neutral expression 'production per unit of input of labour' for 'productivity' and 'labour productivity'.

2. ORIGINALITY

To avoid bringing out old theories, a better knowledge of earlier authors is required. Far too often in economics, conclusions that were already formulated a long time ago are drawn triumphantly. Ignorance – even among well-known authors – is not always the only explanation. Sometimes plagiarism is committed without the least compunction. In this connection, P.A. Sorokin speaks of 'amnesia' and the 'discoverer's complex'. He writes: 'The younger generation of sociologists and psychologists', (and he could just as well have added economists), 'explicitly claims that nothing important has been discovered in their field during all the preceding centuries; . . . and that the real scientific era . . . began only in the last two or three decades with the publication of their own researches . . .'.(14) Hence, the definition of the historian of economic thought as a 'Sadist who delights in pointing out to graduate students and colleagues that their brilliant ideas are not original'.(15)

I have therefore endeavoured – often by numerous quotations – to disclaim originality concerning what has already been said by others.

By this I do not mean that only original works are of value; the desire for originality leads not only to plagiarism, voluntary or involuntary, but also to many publications that should never have seen the light of day. In this respect, G.J. Stigler is right when he states:

> that we commonly exaggerate the merits of originality in economics – that we are unjust in conferring immortality upon the authors of absurd theories while we forget the fine, if not particularly original, work of others.(16)

Vauvenargues was correct in stating that 'It is easier to put forward new ideas than to conciliate those advanced earlier'.(17)

3. IDEOLOGY

Marxists in particular have repeatedly charged that economics is at the service of liberal concepts and that it nurtures extreme individualism and anti-interventionism. In particular, they have in mind hypotheses such as perfect competition, upon which many economic theories are based. This does not, of course, connote economists who because of '. . . their connection with definite parties and pressure groups . . . shut their eyes to the remoter consequences of the policies they are advocating',[18] but the practitioners of economic science who are not at the service of any interest group.

Marx himself upbraided economists for being the scientific representatives of the bourgeoisie.[19] G. Myrdal points out the value judgments that have existed in economic literature since the early physiocrats. These value judgments determine the choice of both the problems treated and the method applied. Myrdal would like every personal preference to be expressed as such, rather than as the result of a nonevaluative economic analysis.[20] In other words, a neutral science is out of the question; F.L. Polak also holds that opinion.[21] P. Dieterlen is no less decisive: 'The economist is an ideologist who accepts or fights himself as such, but then ignores himself. The *no* with which he answers the ideologists around him is neither more nor less ideological than their *yes*'.[22] Other contemporary economists such as K. Boulding[23] and R. Harrod[24] also acknowledge value judgments.[25] According to the Soviet official textbook on economics, a neutral economic science does not exist; economics is a party science: '. . . only a political economy which upholds the interests of the working class can . . . be objective and disinterested'.[26]

Most economists admit that observations are being influenced not only by the intrinsic characteristics of the observed phenomena, but also–unconsciously–by the mirror (our view of the world and society) through which we see the world. Thus, observations may also be influenced by social bias and education.[27] In other words, they accept the existence of an ideological bias, 'though, like Marx, they find it only in others and never in themselves; but they do not admit that it is an inescapable curse and that it vitiates economics to its core.'[28] Seeing value judgments always and everywhere makes any objective knowledge impossible. If the choice of certain subjects of study or hypotheses,[29] and the emphasis that is laid on the analysis, can eventually or immediately be explained by ideological and psychological factors, this does not mean that their scientific significance is thereby impaired. They must 'in any case . . . be judged independently of those subjective elements, and according to their own tendency'.[30] Ideological factors may indeed be stimulating. K.R. Popper even argues that 'The objective and neutral scientist . . . is not the ideal scientist. Being a scientist without motivation is no good, not even in exact sciences'.[31] Divergent points of view are not necessarily due to value judgments:

> . . . often a certain unavoidable allowance for divergent personal opinions exists . . . because it is impossible to determine all relevant, and for the solution of the problem necessary, facts and relations. But then, the researchers' subjective latency is not the primary cause of such differences of opinion.[32]

According to the generally accepted view, economic science does not become involved in the definition of targets; it takes them for granted and only says how they must be achieved.[33] Prominent among those who plead for a nonevaluative economic analysis is Max Weber.[34] The critics mentioned above call this neutrality ethically objectionable: It is alleged to imply indifference to society.[35] However, this overlooks the difference between economic science and its application. Every economist has the right to have his or her own opinion on the targets of economic policy. Nevertheless, the economist is expected to state his or her value judgments clearly. A socialist and a liberal economist pursue differing aims; what one of them accepts as normal is unacceptable to the other. But liberal and socialist or Marxist economies are nonexistent.

Welfare theory sets out to study value judgments and facts in combination. The practitioners of welfare theory, who do not necessarily accept that it is part of the economist's task to state the aims of economic policy, nevertheless maintain that economics must decide which economic system will yield maximum utility or maximum welfare. A. Smith maintained that this would result from the free exchange of production factors; by seeking profits each individual helps to maximize the common good (by the working of the 'invisible hand').[36] Later on, V. Pareto proved this mathematically,[37] but proceeding from rather unrealistic hypotheses (e.g. perfect competition, a stationary economy and a given income distribution, no social wants).[38] Under perfect competition, there is no point in changing the distribution of goods: Prices of goods vary with their marginal productivity. A change in income would lessen the satisfaction of at least one consumer or the output of at least one producer. Numerous authors have elaborated on welfare theory, but since they have further exposed its unreality, little can be done with their directives. Thus, the Pareto theorem is only valid for a given income distribution. Since one cannot prove that any given distribution is better than any other, welfare theory assumes that government will establish a scale of social preferences, which is supposed to aggregate the preferences of the whole community. But this assumption disregards social wants, and also the view that some wants should be discouraged and others encouraged.[39] Welfare theory is of little practical value. Even if, for instance, we knew all those who would benefit or be harmed by a certain measure (which we do not), it would still be impossible to compare subjective judgments of the burdens and benefits concerned (interpersonal utility comparisons being impossible). Hence, F.A. Lutz's remark: 'It is . . . no miracle that only a handful of English theorists concern themselves with this side of welfare economics'.[40]

In recent times, more and more voices have been calling for a more active approach by the economist. The latter is required to be involved in current problems. More specifically, the economist is expected to be interested in the reformation of present-day society. 'Today's fashion often hesitates between two opinions difficult to reconcile: arguing in favour of involvement but against scientists having their hands tied'.[41] Indeed, the two generally go together. F. Hartog rightly points out that there is no danger of a lack of 'involvement', but of a 'critical distance from which, free of all attachments, only the truth is aimed at'. He therefore argues in favour of a 'free, critical, fundamental and objective study of science in general and of economics in particular'.[42] From what has just been stated it follows that this attitude is not easy to adopt. More than any other science, economics must guard against the influence of political convictions on theory.

2 THE THEORY OF THE CONSUMER'S BEHAVIOUR

Since the theory of the consumer's behaviour is founded mainly on Gossen's 'laws' or on the indifference curves, these are discussed first, followed by demand and the consumption and saving functions.

1. GOSSEN'S 'LAWS'

Gossen's 'laws' are to a great extent unrealistic because the consumer does not know the amount of the marginal utility – not measurable – yielded by the consumption of the last unit of a good (quite apart from whether or not the concept is familiar). Exceptions to the first 'law' (marginal utility declines as more units are added) are not infrequent; for instance, if one drinks a second glass of beer immediately after the first then the second may provide greater utility than the first.

The second law states that the marginal utilities of the goods purchased must be proportional to the outlays needed to acquire them.

But the consumer has only imperfect knowledge of the prices of different goods. And in any case, no scholarly comparison of marginal utilities is made. It would, in fact, be difficult to attain equality in the ratios because of the limited divisibility or the indivisibility of most goods. Yet the consumer unconsciously aims at equal ratios.

Much of the consumer's behaviour is the result of traditions and habits determined by social environment; however, this does not necessarily have adverse consequences as it enables the consumer to reduce his transaction costs (e.g. for clothes).(1) The consumer normally adheres to a set pattern of consumption, but changes in prices or in income do exercise a certain influence. Some purchases may be motivated by impulse or emotion (e.g. when the consumer buys goods impulsively). In that case, as J. Marchal has put it, the consumer is much more 'l'homme de Pavlov' than 'l'homme de Descartes'.(2) The consumer only takes time to buy a limited number of goods (usually expensive goods for which he or she is willing to incur high transaction costs), and is also influenced by incidentals. On the other hand, money may be spent liberally on commodities such as makeup.

Moreover, when a consumer purchases various goods, the situation or the opinion of the other consumers is constantly taken into consideration. Greater satisfaction of wants is no synonym for greater (total) utility or more happiness; if satisfaction of the wants of others has increased to a greater extent, the consumer does not have the feeling that total utility has been enhanced. In order to secure greater prestige, one can, on the one hand, aim at wealth and/or political power, or, on the other hand, promote charitable activities.

Utility is a relative, not an absolute, concept. The fact is that interpersonal utility comparison is not possible, precisely because utility is not measurable.

E. Wagemann was not exaggerating when he complained about 'how much ingenuity and trouble has been expended in speculating about marginal utilities'.(3)

2. THE INDIFFERENCE CURVES

To circumvent the difficulty that utility cannot be measured, *indifference curves* are often used. That a consumers' scale of preference is given (and cannot be influenced)—as is assumed in the theory of indifference curves—is not in accordance with reality. Hence, K. Boulding considers the doctrine of 'the Immaculate Conception of the indifference curve' as 'one of the most peculiar illusions of economists'.(4) It is also doubtful whether the consumer can distinguish between the numerous indifferent situations. Indeed, how can the consumer know that two combinations are indifferent, if their utility is not known? The consumer buys the different goods in more or less constant ratios. In any case, there is no point in assuming unlimited substitutability among the goods. The fact that this tool of analysis is not very realistic becomes even clearer when it is extended and used for more than two goods: How could the consumer possibly distinguish between the thousands of possible combinations? In 1932 H. Mayer pointed out:

> The more goods contained in a combination and the more heterogeneous those goods, the more grotesque the consequences that flow from the fiction that as we consume less bread or meat we will consume more salt, that every reduction in the amount of tea consumed is offset by an increase in the amount of sugar consumed in the equivalent (indifferent) daily combinations, the less furniture the more rooms, the less heating material the more aesthetic pleasure, the less clothing the more cigarettes, and so on. More clearly than any abstract argument, these absurd deductions expose the wholly unempirical nature of the supposedly empirical assumptions on which the construction of indifference curves is based.(5)

As with marginal utility, we have to bear in mind the fact that the available money is not necessarily *entirely* spent, and that most goods are indivisible and not homogeneous—still other assumptions on which the doctrine of the indifference curves is based. Indivisibility finds particularly marked expression in the expensive consumption goods of which only one unit is normally purchased (car, refrigerator). Even if a second unit is purchased, the consumer goes for diversity and generally chooses a different model: The neighbours must notice the second acquisition. In fact, not only different commodities are compared but also different qualities of the same commodity (each quality constituting a different product).

Indifference curves are useful only in the analysis of problems of choice of a limited kind (e.g. between present and future consumption, between material possessions and leisure). However, they are not observable phenomena. To obviate this drawback, P.A. Samuelson has suggested[6] basing analysis on consumer preferences as expressed in market conduct, or actual purchases – the theory of revealed preferences. Even here it is very difficult to draw the relevant curves or behaviour lines, since they would have to take account of large variations in income in order to reveal the associated preferences. If compatible with income, durable goods may be bought together or in any order; then nothing is revealed. Moreover, one observation is not sufficient. (The same preference may not result.) Here again, one often forgets that wants are changeable and that the consumer's purchases are determined by habit, not by minor fluctuations in income.

We therefore agree with E.J. Mishan when he describes these theories of the consumer's behaviour as 'an unnecessary adornment on the apparatus of economic analysis'.[7]

3. THE INFLUENCE OF THE OTHER CONSUMERS

As I have pointed out above, there is an interrelationship of the satisfaction of wants of various households. The quantity demanded for a given product sometimes increases because people notice that it is being bought by other consumers, and people are always ready to imitate their fellows. In other cases, the quantity demanded falls when we see other consumers buying a product. (We do not want to imitate and wish to purchase another product.) H. Leibenstein calls these phenomena the 'bandwagon effect' and the 'snob effect'.[8] A 'snob effect' can turn into a 'bandwagon effect'.

They should not be confused with the 'demonstration effect'[9]: When we come into contact with better quality products previously unknown to us, we buy them and our consumption expenditure goes up even if our income has remained unchanged. In point of fact, the bandwagon effect and the demonstration effect usually coincide, because the latter occurs while one is observing other people's consumption.

In this connection we can finally refer to the Veblen effect[10]: Demand increases because price goes up, since the consumer wishes to demonstrate the ability to buy expensive goods (conspicuous consumption).

4. DEMAND

By demand, in economics, we usually mean the series of quantities of a good that we are prepared to buy in the future at a given time or within a specified short period at various (hypothetical) prices.

The construction of demand schedules and demand curves is, however, very difficult. F. Machlup has called the operation a 'tour de force'.[(11)] Indeed, it requires us to establish the reactions of a consumer (or a group of consumers) to the different prices all ruling at the same moment. As this is impossible, we are obliged to rely on assumptions or to study the amounts actually demanded at *different times.* The latter method is dangerous because the other circumstances that are assumed to remain the same change, in fact, even when the period of observation is relatively short.

Even when we obtain satisfactory results, there is nothing to say that our demand curve will not be completely different the following day. It seems hardly likely that the consumer considers what his or her reactions would be if other, hypothetical, prices existed for the innumerable goods available on the market. If this is the case, the consumer will still think in terms of the actual price and investigate only a small number of possibilities with his price forecasts within a limited range (price fluctuations of, say, 10 percent). It is sometimes assumed that the consumer has two limit prices in mind for a restricted number of commodities – a minimum price below which a reliable product could not be supplied, and a maximum price above which the product is too expensive. The demand curve would then consist of a few points only.

Price changes do influence purchases of consumer durables by new consumers, but not so much the purchases of consumers who already possess the product in question. The further the price goes down the more readily will the latter replace durable goods (reducing the period of depreciation); at the same time they will be more likely to move over to a better quality product. The stocks and durability of consumer durables have an important effect on the choice of other goods.

In the demand schedule it is assumed that each price has to be considered as a datum. In other words, the buyer cannot influence the price by his or her purchase (because it represents a very small part of total purchases); this also implies that consumers' decisions are taken independently of each other (pure competition). Some buyers, however, are in a position to exert pressure on sellers; for instance, a cloister community, department stores and other big firms (although here we are examining households' demand, the concept also applies to the firms' demand for intermediate products). Finally, price is only one of the factors that influence demand. Hence, the distinction that is sometimes made, depending on the frequency and nature of purchases, between convenience goods, shopping goods and specialty goods.

Why economists accepted such a far from operational definition of demand (and related concepts such as price elasticity) is an enigma. Consequently, it is not surprising that some authors such as R.E. Emmer[(12)] argue that demand, if defined as above, does not exist.

5. CONSUMPTION AND SAVING

It is often asserted, following J.M. Keynes,[(13)] that the marginal propensity to consume will gradually decline as income increases because saving can be stepped up (this is known as the *absolute income hypothesis*). Consumption does go up as income rises, but not to the same extent. The consumption function, then, is represented by a rising curve gradually flattening out. However, J.S. Duesenberry[(14)] considers that because of the demonstration effect individual preferences cannot be regarded as given: They are affected by the behaviour of other consumers ('keeping up with the Joneses'). In this case, consumption increases in proportion to income; in other words, the consumption curve is a straight line. This 'relative income hypothesis' is also maintained by F. Modigliani.[(15)]

M. Friedman,[(16)] for his part, maintains that saving always represents the same proportion of 'permanent' income and consumption (the '*permanent income hypothesis*'), 'permanent' income including normal prospective income in succeeding periods. Fortuitous and temporary factors can result in lower actual earnings than the expected income (which is very hard to estimate statistically). F. Modigliani stresses 'permanent wealth' rather than 'permanent income' (life cycle theory).

What we said about the demand curve also applies, mutatis mutandis, to the consumption and saving curves: It is difficult to construct these curves. Further, it is simplistic to explain consumption and saving curves mainly by income; they are too much affected by other circumstances that in theory are assumed to remain the same but never do (e.g. the income distribution and relative prices). This explains why empirical inquiries concerning the theories referred to previously have yielded disappointing and contradictory results. The consumption and saving functions are changing constantly, and what is true today may not hold tomorrow.

All this bears out the (still applicable) statement by A.F. Burns some thirty years ago: '. . . our ability to forecast what increment of consumer outlay will accompany a specified increment of income . . . is as yet very limited'.[17]

6. CONCLUSION

The foregoing shows that little is certain about consumer behaviour. One is justifiably surprised that the constant efforts in this field have yielded relatively meagre results.[18] M. Shubik deplores the existing theory being presented '. . . as though it were the relevant way to study consumer behavior, rather than one partially explored path in almost virgin territory.'[19]

3 THE THEORY OF PRODUCER'S BEHAVIOUR

Because many theories are based on the assumption of complete substitutability, this concept will be studied first. After evaluating the optimum combination of factors of production and the optimum level of production, we will discuss supply and the investment decision.

1. SUBSTITUTABILITY AND COMPLEMENTARITY OF PRODUCTION FACTORS

Complete substitutability is nonexistent because factors are not entirely divisible. Machines have fixed capacities. Let us take a plant in which two different machines are needed to produce a certain good. If one has a capacity of 2 cwt, and the other a capacity of 4 cwt, part of the second machine's capacity will be idle if the plant produces 3 cwt. The same holds true of the labour input. In fact, only a limited number of combinations are possible. In the long run as well, complete substitutability does not exist.

Because the assumption of complete substitutability is highly suitable for mathematical analysis (e.g. the Cobb-Douglas production function), most studies proceed on it.

In fact, we find neither complete substitutability nor a constant ratio between the factors of production. The law of variable returns makes this evident. Increasing returns are in a sense explained by the indivisibility of the constant factor: The proportion of one factor to another may not immediately be what is wanted; after the best combination has been achieved, the relationship will again become unsatisfactory. The 'law' simply expresses the fact 'that there is a limit to the extent to which one factor of production can be substituted for another'.[(1)] The validity of the 'law' depends upon the successively added units being homogeneous, and this is not always the case.

2. THE OPTIMUM COMBINATION OF FACTORS FOR A GIVEN LEVEL OF OUTPUT

Where factors are substitutable, the cheapest of the possible combinations for producing a given quantity must be selected. The cheapest combination is that at which the marginal productivity of each additional unit of money spent on the factors is the same. If different additional sums (always assumed to be marginal) are spent, then the respective marginal productivities should be proportional to them. When we are considering two factors alone, then the optimum combination can be found by means of *isoquants* (a curve which represents different combinations of the factors of production yielding the same quantity of output[(2)].)

Since marginal productivities are difficult to calculate and isoquants even more difficult to work out, this method does not provide much of a basis on which to determine the optimum combination of factors. Moreover, the incomplete divisibility of factors limits its validity.

Longer term considerations can also play a part. When, for example, the speed with which a specified volume of production can be reached is considered important, entrepreneurs in less-developed countries are sometimes obliged to have recourse to capital-intensive methods. This may also be warranted if the firm can count on a wide market.

The theory also assumes that a change in the price of one factor has no influence on the price of another factor. However, this is not the case.

In point of fact, firms generally go by trial and error—starting out from an existing set of circumstances and seeing what happens when they make a (small) change in the combination of factors—or else they rely on experience built up by other firms. In certain cases, it is also possible to make use of linear programming (whenever there is a linear relationship between input and production, as is sometimes the case).

3. OPTIMUM LEVEL OF PRODUCTION

According to current economic theory we must determine the additional revenue and additional cost of producing an additional infinitesimal quantity. As long as marginal revenue is greater than marginal cost, increasing output will increase profits (at least in the rising part of the marginal cost curve). We therefore continue to produce up to the point where marginal cost equals marginal revenue.

Marginal cost and marginal revenue are, however, difficult to calculate, and—furthermore—the majority of entrepreneurs are not conversant with the concepts. So the entrepreneur would have to compare the total revenue and the total cost corresponding to each level of production. Where the difference is greatest, he or she no longer has any interest in expanding production. In practice, however, the optimum level of output *sold* is generally established from the gross profits per unit (the difference between the selling price and the variable costs per unit).

The production level is then regarded as a function of sales. Methods of computing the optimum sales level include break-even point analysis and direct costing—the two not being mutually exclusive. In certain cases it is also possible to make use of linear programming.

Break-even analysis does not indicate the level of production that yields maximum profits. It only gives us an idea of the amount the firm must sell so that gross profits per unit equal average fixed costs. And even then we must not lose sight of the fact that the total revenue curve in particular is difficult to estimate. Finally, this method can only be applied easily where output is homogeneous. For heterogeneous production, direct costing is the method commonly employed.

The great advantage of direct costing lies in the fact that there is no allocation of fixed costs; this in itself produces a considerable saving of labour. Where it is not so important to know the cost price (because direct costing is only a partial cost-price calculation), that is, in plants that have no need to worry about profits or whose production and sales do not vary widely, this method is to be recommended. Whenever an accurate knowledge of cost is wanted (custom work or unit production), then absorption costing is indicated. However, the two methods can be combined.

In practice it is not easy to determine the optimum level of production. If we apply break-even analysis, we have to estimate future revenue, as we must with direct (standard) costing too. Pricing is therefore of the greatest importance; normally, the aim should be to maximize profits. Profit- seeking, however, is not always the primary consideration in running a business. And many entrepreneurs' decisions (like those of the consumer) are questions of pure habit. This is especially true of frequently repeated purchases and those involving a small outlay. Personal feelings and reactions play their part, too.

4. SUPPLY AND REVENUE

Like the demand curve, the supply curve is extremely difficult to construct (partly because the other things assumed to be equal do not in fact remain equal). Here, too, potential reactions will be examined over a limited price range only. Since prices are regarded as given, the supply schedule holds good only in the case of pure competition. Moreover, lags are being ignored. The elasticity of supply is even more difficult to determine than that of demand, and it has not been studied as thoroughly.

Bearing in mind the remarks on demand, we need not be surprised that the concept of the average revenue curve does not lead very far in practice. The supplier should be guided by an estimated curve and has, in fact, no concrete data to draw on in making this estimate. In view of the supplier's uncertainty, he or she should start rather from a demand or sales zone. Generally, however, the supplier does not know all these concepts. In the end, the quantities sold do not depend on price alone, and in many cases the price is not even a decisive factor. When the output of a monopolistic enterprise increases, a fall in prices is not inevitable, because in many cases we have to deal with administered prices.

5. THE INVESTMENT DECISION

Entrepreneurs often rely on methods that amount to working out the expected return on an investment. In the present value calculation and internal rate of return method, the assessment of an investment project is determined mainly by the estimated revenues and by the target rate of interest, the latter depending on both the market rate of interest and the ratio of owned to borrowed capital. The payoff method also amounts to an estimate of the rate of interest, which in most cases is high. Applied to one and the same investment project, the first two methods will produce the same result.

The difficulty lies in estimating future returns—not only their annual level but also how long they will accrue. At an interest rate of 50 percent, a four-year forecast is sufficient. Estimates that are reliable or at all accurate are generally impossible to obtain. This explains the success of the relatively simple payoff method. If, however, the entrepreneur asks too much in respect of the payoff period (the period is taken too short), he or she runs the risk of lagging behind technological advance (by not proceeding to the investment). The preference for a short payoff period springs from the fact that entrepreneurs can anticipate the movement of certain factors for only a limited period.

Experience shows that the influence of the rate of interest on investment decisions, particularly the decisions of established concerns, is relatively slight. It appears to increase only when the rate is high (say, 10 percent or more). The investment programmes (and reserves) of large firms run to a number of years and are not influenced by small interest rate fluctuations.

Generally speaking, the theory being applied does not take into account the stock of capital goods. If the entrepreneur considers his or her stock of capital goods sufficient, then the entrepreneur will not invest, whatever the rate of interest. This might make us claim that there is a closer link between investment and the desired stock of capital goods than between investment and interest (a decision to invest is often made simply because it proves technically necessary); to check the accuracy of such a claim is quite a problem because the appropriate size of capital goods stocks is difficult to establish.

Other factors are of great importance to the investment decision – changes in technological knowledge, the growth rate of demand, the probable trend of costs (fluctuations in the price of production factors), the attitude of government (tax policy). One must also consider the reactions of other producers: If their market share is threatened, they too will make efforts to invest – which may result in excess capacity. The pursuit of greater power and psychological motives may also play a role.

All this shows that the entrepreneur's investment decision cannot normally be based on a few simple criteria: Too many subjective elements come into play. It is unwise to cover risk by increasing the target rate of interest or reducing the payoff period without good reason; it is much more advisable to build up general reserves. For the most part, deciding what investment should be made is still what A. I. Diepenhorst calls a refined form of fortune telling.[(3)]

6. CONCLUSION

From what has been said it follows that the theory in application is not in line with the true facts: 'The real world still escapes our models . . . we wonder whether economics can . . . continue to ignore the actual decision-making processes of real firms'.[(4)]

4 THE THEORY OF PRICING

In this chapter, marginalism and two of its basic assumptions will be discussed. Finally, some comments will be made on price interdependence and the laws of supply and demand.

1. MARGINALISM

According to marginal price theory, the entrepreneur attempts to equate marginal cost and marginal revenue in order to maximize profits. However, firms actually employ other methods in pricing. In general, entrepreneurs apparently do not even know these marginal concepts.

The marginal method does not determine whether fixed costs, and hence average total costs, are covered. So this requires further examination. Sales promotion costs, moreover, are given little weight. While the technique proceeds as though producers and consumers were in direct contact, this is rarely the case. Frequently, it is even the wholesaler who actually sets prices. Marginal costs (especially in the long term) and above all marginal revenue cannot as a rule be calculated, and the countless attempts to determine the demand curve empirically have been unsuccessful (see Chapters 2, section 4).

One of the other objections to marginalism is that it attaches no importance to stability considerations. It assumes that changes in marginal cost and revenue are immediately reflected in changes in price. The continuous price fluctuations that result, however, encourage speculation. Both dealers and consumers prefer price stability, which also makes it easier for firms to plan ahead. In other words, it is often better to let a short-term advantage go in order to safeguard long-term interests (inter alia with an eye to potential competition, which may come from either new or existing firms). What are known as *administered prices* meet these requirements.

In addition, there may be objection to the marginal method on the grounds that it establishes the most profitable level of output (not price). In reality, the business executive first sets his price; only then does he or she consider what quantity it will be possible to sell. In determining this quantity, marginal theory does not even make allowance for the need to use as much as possible of the capacity available. It is in no way concerned with unused capacity (because fixed costs are not taken into account).

A detailed critique of the marginal price theory cannot be given here (I will not engage in vague and romantic criticism, as exemplified by the remark sometimes made that marginalism would be 'antirevolutionary'). In addition, it may be mentioned that when higher prices are ascribed to monopolistic competition and oligopoly rather than to pure competition, this applies only if the cost curves remain unchanged. Greater output on the other hand, generally brings costs down.

Let us take oligopoly, a prevalent market structure. Following accepted hypotheses concerning both the aims of the firm concerned and its competitors' reactions, numerous divergent theories can be developed. The term *oligopoly,* in fact, covers highly divergent market situations; some oligopolies, for instance, involve three competitors, others twenty. The size of the firms may vary. Oligopolies may be homogeneous or heterogeneous, uncoordinated or coordinated. Consequently, it is not easy to formulate a general statement, and the lack of a satisfactory theory is not surprising. Hence, M. Shubik states: 'There is no oligopoly theory. There are bits and pieces of models'.(1) Oligopoly is 'the real blind spot in price theory',(2) 'a disturbing and recalcitrant problem, especially to the mathematically minded theorist, who insists upon having "the answer"'(3), and T. Seitz correctly points out that 'theoretically based statements about oligopolistic price leadership are only possible to a very limited extent'.(4)

The real drawbacks to the marginal theory of price, however, are the two major assumptions on which it rests; although it is mentioned incidentally that business executives can have objectives other than profit maximization, it is assumed that profit maximization is the only important aim; it is also assumed that price and quantity are the business executive's chief policy instruments, even when it is admitted that he or she may sometimes have others to rely upon. We shall deal with these two assumptions in turn.

2. CORPORATE OBJECTIVES

An examination of corporate behaviour is the only means of studying how a firm reaches its decisions. Empirical studies have shown that as a general rule a variety of aims are pursued.

Among the most prominent objectives of major corporations in the United States are a satisfactory (however not a maximal) revenue on investment, stable prices and profit margins, gaining or holding a given market share and meeting or forestalling competition. In Denmark the small firms appear to pursue maximization of profits in the short run while the large firms, though their aims are the same, give more attention to long-term considerations.(5) The behaviour of the small firms is due, in some cases, to a shortage of liquid assets.

W.J. Baumol regards maximizing sales as the foremost objective, at least provided total profits do not fall below a specified minimum.(6) More particularly, the aim should be maximization of the rate of growth of sales. Maximizing sales is a matter of prestige, and a firm will endeavour to preserve or increase its share of the market. At the same time, managers seek to demonstrate their ability, and this may lead to higher salaries in that company or elsewhere[7] (especially in the most common case where they hold little or none of the firm's capital).

Occasionally, the main purpose of the entrepreneur is, especially in independent firms, simply a quiet life. Leisure is preferred over higher profits (upon which higher taxes are imposed), security over more risks, good relations with colleagues over rivalry. This is by no means fanciful: The slow rate of economic growth in some countries may partly be attributed to it.

In many cases, the need for a minimum of liquid assets is in conflict with the target of maximizing profits: A firm usually tries to avoid substantial indebtedness and preserve its independence, hence the preference for self-financing. Moreover, as we have already seen, the avoidance of potential competition is incompatible with a policy directed at maximizing profits. This in fact also applies to firms wishing to maintain good relations with consumers, suppliers, investors, trade unions and above all the government.

Anyway, profit maximization cannot be regarded as the major objective of the firm; other objectives, relating to sales, production and stocks, are by no means subsidiary. The importance of these aims varies from case to case, and no general rules can be formulated here. Within the firm, the various objectives themselves often give rise to conflicts between the heads of different divisions. The determination, persuasiveness, or other qualities of one executive will sometimes turn the scales.

3. INSTRUMENTS OF CORPORATE POLICY

Although they are not the only instruments of marketing policy, almost exclusive attention is given to price and quantity in economic theory. Often, however, price is of subordinate interest, and the other policy instruments such as quality (very often closely related to R & D expenditure), sales promotion, distribution channels and product-line policy, are more important. The extent to which these different instruments (which constitute the marketing mix) are used has not yet been examined very closely. We shall concentrate on these instruments further. The choice of instruments depends first of all on the nature of the goods offered for sale. The financial situation may also be of great significance. There are no general rules. Time and again we see that a firm obtains better results by attaching importance to such items as advertising and packaging rather than by lowering the selling price.

a. Price

Price sensitivity varies from product to product, from consumer to consumer. There are many goods (or types of good) for which the consumer pays little attention to price; on the other hand, there are others for which price is of great significance. Consumers comparing prices (over a certain period, and at the same moment but in different shops), are less numerous than is generally supposed. Mostly, they are only informed about a limited number of prices.

Price increases are not to be condemned out of hand. They can be explained as being due to improved quality or greater demand. In certain cases (even for homogeneous goods), however, firms systematically price their products above their competitors' (this is made possible by product differentiation) to create the impression that they are offering better quality. Due to the (largely irrational) behaviour of consumers, insignificant changes are often made to a product in order to sell it at a higher price (product variation).

Price reductions are sometimes believed to signify a decline in quality, an unsuccessful line, difficulties in maintaining liquidity, or the imminent introduction of a new model. A price cut may, in fact, appreciably reduce sales of a product, when a certain class of consumer is attracted precisely because of its price.

b. Quality

This is a concept that can cover industrial design, packaging, servicing, delivery times and product variation. For many goods and services (dry cleaning, for instance) price is not as important as quality and speedy delivery. The quality of durable goods is often kept low deliberately in order to make them wear out sooner and thus promote replacement purchases. When the consumer is accustomed to a price that is a good round figure, the quality (or the weight) of a product (e.g. a bar of chocolate) is often reduced as an alternative to increasing the price (a practice known as *price line pricing*). Packaging and servicing are becoming steadily more important. This also applies to product variation. It is no simple matter to determine optimum quality and the corresponding selling price.

c. Sales Promotion

Sales promotion is the practice whereby firms employ representatives and advertising to inform dealers and consumers of the qualities of their products and to encourage them to buy. The word is used in its narrower sense here, since price and quality are also means of stimulating sales.

Advertising, in addition to its useful function of providing information, can force prices up. In many cases, advertising does not increase a firm's market share because of the compensatory effect of advertising by competing firms. Firms are often put out of business by competitors whose products are inferior but who put a bigger effort into sales promotion.

d. Distribution

A firm can see to the distribution of its own products or can give the job to outsiders. Everything here depends on the consumers to be reached, the need to provide information (e.g. with consumer durables) and the type and status of the product. Prestige, for example, will probably rule out distribution through chain stores, although it must be borne in mind that these are becoming increasingly important.

The main drawback to distribution through independent retail firms, in fact, lies in the margin competition resulting from resale price maintenance – competition shifts from the consumer to the distributor. As the retailer stimulates sales of the most profitable products, the producer tends to set prices at a level that permits distribution margins at least equal to or, preferably, higher than those granted by his or her competitors. This tendency explains the possibility of 'rebate wars' (especially during a depression).

e. Product Range

Industrial and, to an even greater extent, commercial firms are often constrained to increase the number of types of goods they produce – in other words, to widen their product range. This strengthens their bargaining position vis-à-vis competitors with only a few products and vis-à-vis the distributors handling their products.

4. PRICE INTERDEPENDENCE

The application of the theory of price interdependence has not yielded the results that were originally expected. It is no longer accepted that a system of simultaneous equations with the same number of equations as unknowns will yield an equilibrium solution (no forces at work to upset the equilibrium). Equality is neither a sufficient nor a necessary condition for the existence of a solution (even for the existence of one single solution). Attempts have accordingly been made in recent years to determine the conditions for a general equilibrium. So far, these have all been based on perfect or pure competition (and other unrealistic hypotheses, such as a constant number of economic units and goods produced, no returns to scale, no externalities, stability of the consumers' preferences, etc.). The statement of U. Ricci on the theory of general equilibrium is still valid: 'a marvellous castle . . . but of no help in solving the housing problem'.[(8)]

5. THE 'LAWS' OF SUPPLY AND DEMAND

The 'laws' of supply and demand are questionable as well. A variation in demand will virtually always elicit a change in supply and, conversely, a variation in supply a change in demand. Rising demand may thus be conducive to an increase in supply, where the additional output affords a reduction in the cost price. In this event there is no price increase, and there may even be a reduction.

Thus, all possibilities are left open, and little use can be derived from the 'laws' of supply and demand. Hence, there is reinforcement for R. Harrod's contention that they will play only a minor part in the 'economics of the future'.[(9)] Price expectations, moreover, may lead to opposite reactions, which brings A. Lowe to the conclusion that 'such volatility of expectations . . . disconfirms the Law of Supply and Demand . . .'[(10)] and one can agree with G. Tarde's view that prices are determined by opinion rather than by the law of supply and demand.[(11)]

6. CONCLUSION

We need not be surprised that there has been much criticism of the theory of pricing. J. Robinson somewhat exaggeratedly complains that 'economic science has not yet solved its first problem – what determines the price of a commodity?'[(12)] The theory of pricing only provides us with '. . . either some common generalities . . . or an abundance of complicated but useless theories . . .'[(13)] it is 'devoid of specific substantive content'.[(14)] Power relationships are not taken into consideration. And A.R. Oxenfeldt justifiably states: 'The detailed analysis of prices . . . suggests that every price is unique in some important respect. No fairly simple explanation of price, like the law of supply and demand, has been uncovered'.[(15)]

Business executives who do not adhere to the rules of marginalism are no wiser as a result of the application of the full standard cost price. The latter merely indicates the minimum selling price in the long run; in the short term this function is performed by the variable standard cost price. It does not indicate the level at which the selling price should be set (for demand must be considered), and here, as previously shown, the producer has no firm data to go on. This explains why experts agree that setting prices is more of an art than a science. In certain cases – price discrimination or a slump – products may be sold at a loss; many factories produce different commodities to which varying margins are applied; profits are greater on one article than on another, according to the (fluctuating) potential of the market. New products especially can sometimes be priced far above cost, as was the case with the first ballpoint pens. Psychological considerations also play a part: Consumers are, for instance, more sensitive to a price increase from \$0.95 to \$1.05 than to a rise from \$0.75 to \$0.85.

5 THE THEORY OF INCOME DISTRIBUTION

The customary theory of distribution is greatly influenced by marginal theory. According to this theory, the first principle underlying demand for factors of production is that the factors' marginal productivities should be in proportion to the sums paid for them. In the demand for a given factor, therefore, the price of the other factors must be taken into consideration if an optimal combination of factors is to be realized.

Further, marginal costs are always compared with marginal revenue. As long as the marginal revenue yielded by the marginal production is greater than the marginal cost, it is advantageous, say, to introduce an additional quantity of capital.

The unrealistic nature of the marginal theory has already been indicated. Marginal costs and revenue are here likewise difficult to calculate. This is also the case whenever the productivity of labour and capital goods must be compared. Labour productivity is moreover linked to the nature of the capital goods at its disposal. Thus, the productivity of a worker may be low because he or she is employed in a labour-intensive industry. Marginal theory assumes homogeneous units; this is true only for a small part of the labour supply (unskilled workers). Finally, no account is taken of power relationships and traditions. The following passage deals with the labour market and the market for loanable funds.

1. THE LABOUR MARKET

Today's labour market usually displays a bilateral monopolistic character in which one or more trade unions negotiate with one or more employers' associations to fix uniform wages in each industry. To determine in advance what wages will result is not possible, since this depends on strength of character, the competence of the negotiators, their insight into the respective bargaining positions, public opinion and the entrepreneur's fear of a substitute product gaining ground in the event of a strike.

Social, political and psychological factors are becoming as important as purely economic considerations. The growth of production per employee, the cost of living and profits are, however, taken into account; the wages in key industries and the competitiveness of the economy (degree of dependence on foreign trade) also exert an influence. When negotiations between employees and employers prove fruitless, the government is often compelled to play the role of arbitrator. In some countries, where a continual supply of new workers is available (through a rapid increase in the population or immigration), and when nonunion workers are prepared to work for a lower wage, government intervention will yield fewer results.

Little help is offered by supply and demand curves. The explanation offered by the marginal theory of distribution is especially weak with respect to supply; labour is supplied until the increasing reluctance to work becomes greater than the decreasing marginal utility of the wage; one loses sight of the possibility of actual job satisfaction. Eventually, the worker prefers leisure to an increase in income and makes greater use of educational facilities. Then we have a backward sloping supply curve. In the industrialized countries the concept of 'supply' loses its significance (quite apart from the objections that have been raised in this connection – regarding demand also), because the quantity offered is determined by institutional circumstances. Working hours are fixed by the government, and overtime is permitted only under certain conditions.

Uncertainty also surrounds the relationship between wages and unemployment, and the Phillips Curve (according to which full employment and a stable level of wages and prices cannot be pursued at the same time) cannot be accepted unreservedly. The Phillips Relation is, for instance, applicable rather to the past century and the beginning of the twentieth century than to recent decades, more to the less-developed than to the developed countries. During the past few years a relatively high unemployment percentage has been accompanied by steep increases in wages and prices (stagflation). Even when the theory is adjusted by proceeding not from nominal but from real fluctuations in wages and prices, the lack of coherence between wages or prices on the one hand, and the unemployment percentage on the other hand, is not explained satisfactorily. According to A. Woll, the Phillips Relation has no significance in the long run, yet it may operate temporarily.[(1)]

Unemployment is not a determining factor of the wage level in the industrialized countries, though it does influence negotiations between employers and employees. The negotiating power of the unions is indeed stronger in times of full employment.

a. Unions and the Wage Level

While some authors, such as M. Friedman,[(2)] minimize the impact of the unions on wage determination, others do not agree with this attitude. Both points of view are backed by statistical evidence. This generally relates to the United States, but what holds good for the United States is not necessarily applicable to Western Europe or to the less-developed countries. Taking his stand particularly on American research, J. Wemelsfelder believes that '. . . from the figures . . . an important influence of the unions on wage determination cannot be deduced'.[(3)] Since 1890, there seems to have been a high degree of correlation between the fluctuations of labour productivity and of real wages. A similar relation has been observed between the trend of wage costs per unit of product and that of wholesale prices. (In other words, prices are regularly adjusted and profits are not impaired.) Wage trends in sectors where the unions are strongly organized have been practically the same as in those sectors where representation of trade unions is weak.

However, one cannot deny that unions, especially in Western Europe, have often succeeded in obtaining increases in real wages, mainly in the concentrated sectors. This is often indicated by the share of wages and salaries in the national income. Unions go on securing wage increases – in a certain sense they are obliged to do so to justify their activity – but employers do not worry about it a great deal as long as they are able to pass these increases on in the selling price (and provided the competitiveness of those countries which are dependent on exports makes this possible). Both groups often negotiate at the expense of the consumer. While employers and unions represent powerful pressure groups – and for the moment unions are certainly the most powerful – the same cannot be said of the consumers. Wage increases, which hamper firms' investment efforts, are counter-productive. During recent years this seems to have been the case in many countries.

The customary theory does not consider the fact that the trade union cannot be considered as a purely economic organization. To justify its activity to its members, wage increases are sought during periods in which this is not desirable (because inflation is stimulated) and in which the competitive position of domestic enterprises compares unfavourably with that of firms in other countries. The common good is often considered of little importance (as has repeatedly been seen in the United Kingdom: Technological advance and even the abolition of obsolete functions are opposed). Between November 1969 and April 1970, a London container port was kept idle under pressure of the unions. (In the meantime the cargoes were unloaded in Rotterdam.)

Generally speaking, unions neglect the interests of managerial staff, who are to a larger extent subjected to the adverse effects of inflation (decrease of the real disposable income through progressive taxation). Hence the creation of unions for such staff in some countries.

Typical of present-day trade unionism is the trend towards involvement in all possible fields. Sometimes, under trade union pressure agreements are concluded on matters that are really the government's concern. Thus, in the early 1970s FIAT's management took on the task of creating 12,000 jobs in Southern Italy.) Not only do the unions aspire to the institution of an economic and social democracy, they also have something to say about, for instance, education and culture, national defence, land use planning, housing, aid to the less-developed countries and foreign policy. On the whole, union members are far more interested in improving their own material welfare than in the ideological conflict; as a Dutch union leader put it: 'One does not become member of a trade union to be turned into a political animal by a small group of intellectuals who consider themselves the political élite'.[4] A consequence of this all-embracing action of trade union leaders is a lack of contact with the grassroots members, who are then influenced by extreme-left groups who (successfully) instigate wildcat strikes.

In various countries (e.g. the United States and France) the results of the elections prove that any programme aiming at a more equitable distribution of income and wealth does not appeal to many trade union members (especially in the United States); it is considered a burden on the working population, from which the inactive part of the population derives the benefit.

Frequently, the joint councils of government representatives, workers' and employers' organizations argue about (or even decide upon) matters that are the province of parliaments. (Even in his day, Bismarck looked upon the Prussian 'Volkswirtschaftsrat' as an instrument to reduce the authority of Parliament).

There is a need for much more research concerning the influence exercised by the union: '. . . the precise role of unions and institutions remains an open question'.[5]

b. Wage Differentials

It is difficult to find an explanation for wage differences in every case. In the same groups and in the same places differences exist (between men's and women's wages). One must take into account the varying degrees of power among unions, a factor that is itself associated with the varying profit positions among industries and firms. Thus, in the same industries the wages often vary depending on the district. Usually, the higher the concentration of production, the better the wages are in the industries concerned. Different wages are often paid for the same work. Demographic pressure also influences this common phenomenon.

It frequently happens that the same, or only a slightly different, wage is paid for different performances. Normally the potential to raise wages is determined by the trend of production per man-hour. Hence, in some industries it is possible for wages to rise faster. But workers in other sectors where the rate of growth of productivity is not so high, or even nonexistent (education, medical care, manual labour, theatre, restaurants, hairdressers) want to maintain existing wage differentials. This is why wages and prices in many service industries have risen so fast that they can no longer be paid (e.g. domestic staff) or that their quality suffers consequently (e.g. crowded classes, restaurants).

In spite of the attempts that have been made to determine the optimal wage differences scientifically, the wages structure is still governed not only by the scarcity of labour but also by habit and tradition. What A. Ross says of the United States—'The "national wage structure" seems to consist of little islands of rationality in a sea of anarchy'[(6)]—is equally valid for other countries.

2. THE MARKET FOR LOANABLE FUNDS

According to customary theory the interest rate is particularly determined by investments and hoarding on the demand side, and by savings and (additional) money supply on the supply side. This explanation is valid only in the long run and in the absence of monopolistic tendencies and government intervention. Since in the market for loanable funds there is no question of pure competition, it is not possible to determine the interest level by means of the supply and demand curves (which imply pure competition).

Just as in the labour market, various submarkets appear; in fact, there is no such thing as *the* interest rate. Demand for liquidities depends inter alia upon the level of future income (e.g. from real assets) and the moment at which it becomes available, expenditure (the greater the uncertainty in this connection, the higher the demand), the expected price trends (however, the motives for holding cash balances can be so compelling that people are prepared to accept the consequences of inflation), the already acquired property and the cost of converting financial into real assets (and vice versa). Financial institutions continually adapt the structure of their assets to changing circumstances (prices, interest, expectations of future developments); households only do this occasionally. The multitude and the complexity of the factors influencing demand for cash balances makes it difficult to determine such demand. The same is true for investments in securities. This involves many possibilities, and the question as to which assets are to be preferred is not easily answered, partly because future returns are difficult to estimate. Considerations regarding increased risk and the stability of the real value (avoidance of the consequences of inflation) are also relevant. Because of the difficulty of finding precise criteria, F.H. Hahn's statement is not surprising: 'It might well be argued that in situations in which rational behaviour is so difficult individuals will adopt rules of thumb'.(7) Demand for loanable funds in order to invest in capital goods and stocks is dependent on the internal rate of return and perhaps even more on the desired stock of capital goods. The interest rate exerts only a slight influence on investment (see Chapter 3). Thus, the demand for investment purposes may rise in spite of an increase in interest if the profit expectations rise even faster. Similarly, demand may decrease notwithstanding a cut in interest.

Regarding supply, the consequences of fluctuations in interest rates are very small with respect to low and high income. In the first case, the returns are in any event of little importance, and in the second case, savings take on a residual character, regardless of the interest rate. With respect to the middle incomes, savings are normally a fixed proportion of income, which is also little influenced by changes in interest (see Chapter 2). Other considerations are sometimes weightier, such as stability of the value of the assets acquired.

Just as the money supply and liquidity preference are the most decisive elements in the money market, so are saving and investment in the capital market. Though interest appears to exert little influence on either of them, saving and investment have a greater repercussion on the level of interest.

At the moment, the market for loanable funds is more flexible than the labour market, this being due to the influence of international capital movements. These prevent governments of western countries from making use of certain instruments of monetary policy: The freedom of capital movements hampers the efficacy of these measures. That general pronouncements in connection with interest are extremely difficult is a point that also holds good for these international capital movements. Capital exports to Switzerland, for example, are explained not by a higher rate of interest but by greater confidence in the Swiss currency.

As has already been stressed, it is very difficult to make comprehensive judgments on interest. However, it is going too far to say that '. . . the rate of interest can be forgotten, at least in aggregative analysis',(8) and G. L. S. Shackle is surely exaggerating when he concludes a 'survey' of the theories on interest as follows:

> It seems likely that the interest rate, or the system of rates, will continue to receive from theoreticians the homage due to a ceremonial monarch, without in fact counting for more than such a monarch in the real affairs of western nations'.(9)

The theory of interest remains one of the most difficult and debatable areas of economic science:

> The theory of interest has for a long time been a weak spot in the science of economics, and the explanation and determination of the interest rate still gives rise to more disagreement among economists than any other branch of general economic theory.(10)

Although the whole range of interest rates usually moves in the same direction, this is not necessarily the case; neither do they rise or fall in the same proportion. The business cycle has an effect: In a recession, for example, the spread is greater than during a boom and the interest on the money market can even exceed that on the capital market.

The interest structure itself is not very clear: Even the specialist first has to make all sorts of calculations in order to find the actual interest rates. Divergent conditions (e.g. in the case of issue or redemption of bonds), or deliberate misrepresentation (e.g. with reference to consumer credit or personal loans) mean that only the specialist is able to assess opportunities for investing in securities with real knowledge of the facts. A report by the Organization for Economic Cooperation and Development (OECD) accurately concludes: 'In the present state of affairs, the "market process" in many countries is basically distorted by the fact that the majority concerned are unable to ascertain the real rate'.[11]

International comparison of interest rates is equally difficult since the degree of liquidity and, particularly, taxation vary from one country to another. The higher interest on bonds in continental Europe may, for example, be explained by the fact that the banks there sell directly to the individual through a chain of branches; in the United States and Britain, on the other hand, the issues are placed chiefly in the hands of the institutional investors; there are, in fact, no direct sales to households. If this is taken into account, it is questionable whether there is a great difference in the level of interest.

3. CONCLUSION

Even more than the theories discussed in previous chapters, the theory of income distribution is bedevilled by numerous noneconomic factors that must be considered. Up to now, attempts to integrate these factors into the theory have proved unsuccessful.

6 THE THEORY OF THE GENERAL LEVEL OF NATIONAL INCOME AND OF PRICES

This chapter deals, respectively, with monetary equilibrium and the level of national income, inflation, the quantity theory and the cash-balance theory.

1. MONETARY EQUILIBRIUM AND THE LEVEL OF NATIONAL INCOME

According to the theory of monetary equilibrium, the level of the national income is determined by the link between consumption plus savings ($C + S$) and consumption plus investment ($C + I$), or between (ex ante) savings and investment. The difficulties involved in determining the consumption, savings and investment curves have already been indicated. The process implies ex ante data that are related to expectations and intentions and which cannot be quantified. In a sense, it is assumed that we live in a world where all things can be predicted. Thus, to attempt an explanation of monetary equilibrium (and the level of national income) on the basis of these curves offers little in the way of a solution; the shapes of the curves themselves even require an explanation. In fact, the level of national income depends on numerous elements, such as the quantity and quality of production factors, technological progress and institutional circumstances. These elements *are* reflected in savings and investment, but not in a systematic way. In particular, the trend of national income is explained by the interaction of the investment multiplier and the accelerator. Objections are liable to be raised regarding the use of either concept.

a. The Investment Multiplier

The investment multiplier is difficult to determine statistically. The marginal propensity to consume is not constant; it differs from one population group to another, and the distribution of additional income is unknown. In practice, no distinction can be made between incomes that may or may not be the result of, for example, increased investment. A rise in national income is possible, moreover, without an initial increase in expenditure. This may occur as the result of a redistribution of income (at a disadvantage for those with a low marginal propensity to consume, and at an advantage for those with a high marginal propensity to consume). The multiplier can only be expressed in an economy where there is unemployment.

The (sometimes nearly negligible) results of additional investment are counteracted by a rise in imports as well as by the claims made by the government on part of the additional income (the so-called 'leaks'). Fluctuations in stocks frequently cancel out the multiplier effect.

All this also explains why it is so difficult, in practise, to fix the length to be assigned to the time units or periods in the theory. Knowledge of the production period and of the payment habits of the producers—who, moreover, may differ from industry to industry—is indeed not very accurate. (There may be a considerable difference in time from the moment the income is received to the moment it is spent.)

Particularly where the investment multiplier is applied to macroeconomic questions, the *qualitative* differences that accompany the quantitative changes are often overlooked as well as the fact that in many cases the quantitative changes are merely the result of the qualitative differences. H. Hegeland correctly draws attention to the fact:

> that the multiplier theory loses much of its relevance when applied to social aggregates and that it can be fruitfully applied chiefly to problems of micro-economics, i.e., when applied to the effects of changes in a single stream of expenditure within a limited sector of the economy.(1)

b. The Accelerator

The acceleration theory is valid only while *all* machines are in use (no excess capacity), overtime is excluded, the relation between production factors cannot be altered (unchanged technology), sufficient raw materials and labour are present and the entrepreneurs command the necessary financial means. Since these conditions do not usually all exist simultaneously (the machines, for example, are usually replaced by better ones), the accelerator has minor significance; the attempts to measure the accelerator have yielded few results. This is partially due to the difficulty in distinguishing between autonomous and induced investment (particularly on the macroeconomic level).

In order to explain entrepreneurs' investment behaviour, numerous other factors must be taken into consideration. Future expectations play a particularly important part (a capacity shortage cannot be made up immediately; stocks are utilized instead). Investments are made in capital goods, not related to changes in income (e.g. under pressure of increased real wages), while autonomous investment becomes more important (new inventions, public works). The theory is based upon 'balanced' growth: Income and the stock of capital goods increase in the same proportion. This is not the case. Economic growth, furthermore, is not dependent on capital only.

As in the case of the multiplier, the pitfalls of macroeconomic data must be pointed out. A rise in investment can follow increased consumption in a given sector, while the general level of consumption can nevertheless remain the same. This investment could then erroneously be classified as *autonomous.* The accelerator, therefore, is not adequate for explaining changes in aggregate investment. Only under special circumstances and in the short term is there a proportional relationship between output and the stock of capital goods.

The acceleration principle is less general than the multiplier. Whereas the latter operates in both directions, the acceleration principle is effective only in the upward direction—and then only when the firm concerned is operating at full capacity (in the downward direction only if there is no provision for replacement investment).

c. The Interaction

A statistical determination of the multiplier and the accelerator is, in fact, out of the question: Neither the accelerator nor the multiplier (marginal propensity to consume) remains constant. In a recovery period, for example, the accelerator would have to be very low, since excess capacity is available; it would have to rise rapidly as soon as the economy is working at full capacity. The opposite would have to occur with respect to the multiplier.

Whenever it is logical to include the multiplier in the analysis (recovery), it is less convenient for the accelerator. In the case of full capacity operation, on the other hand, the inclusion of the accelerator in the reasoning is justified, while that of the multiplier is not.

The explanation of income fluctuations through the interaction of the multiplier and the accelerator is purely endogenous. There is some doubt as to whether entrepreneurs base their long-term decisions only on short-term considerations. In most cases exogenous factors play an important role (monetary policy).

2. INFLATION

The continuous overall rise in prices of consumer goods can be explained mainly by the rapid increase in the money supply. This is caused by the fact that the central bank does not (or cannot) counteract overspending (demand-pull inflation). However, this is not the only cause of inflation, as is often suggested.

Autonomous increases in wages, profits, and raw materials (which are not influenced by the former or the present level of demand) also lead to increases in costs and prices, out of which a cost-push inflation develops. Here I have in mind particularly exaggerated claims on the part of the trade unions. The cost push, however, reinforces the demand pull, and vice versa—but the two are difficult to distinguish in a period of expansion. The dangers of cost push vary from country to country, according to competitiveness. When profits provide the basis of a cost push, 'markup inflation' is the term used.

In recent years, inflation has usually been sustained by wage increases in excess of productivity growth. T. Balogh (who was one of Harold Wilson's economic advisors) is categoric on this point: 'It is clear that the inflation in the United States, as in Britain, has been caused by wages rising too fast'.(2)

The drive for higher wages is not only an expression of the union's need to justify its activity, but also of the union members' desire to satisfy greater needs. The government is asked to be more assiduous in attending to collective wants, environmental protection and full employment. This policy involves heavy spending . . . and higher taxes. Everyone tries to shift these taxes on others by demanding higher (gross) incomes or by passing them on in prices. Inflation often seems to be very high in countries with a heavy fiscal burden. However, there are economic limits to raising the proportion of taxes in the national income—but weak governments do not have the courage to resist the demands of various pressure groups.

3. THE TRANSACTIONS EQUATION AND THE QUANTITY THEORY

a. The Transactions Equation of Exchange

The exchange equation, $M^*V^* = P^*T^*$, needs no proof.(3) The goods are exchanged for one another: The money available is equal to the amounts needed to pay for the transactions.

The formula enables us to express any one of the factors as a function of the others ($M^* = P^*T^*/V^*$; $V^* = P^*T^*/M^*$; $P^* = M^*V^*/T^*$; $T^* = M^*V^*/P^*$), though this does not tell us anything about the factors themselves. M^*, for instance is partly determined by the structure of the banking system, V^* is determined by the way the economic units normally make payments, P^* is determined by monopolistic conditions, and T^* is determined by the quality and quantity of the production factors.

The time element is disregarded. Present funds are sometimes used to pay for past transactions, often at prices differing from the current ones. Moreover, M^* is a stock at a point in time (although an average can be calculated for a given period), while T^* is a flow over a period of time.

Remember, there are dangers involved in using aggregated data. As has already been pointed out, various price indices have been compiled on account of the heterogeneity of the various commodities. The 'general' level of prices does not explain the price levels of the different commodity groups, and the influence of a greater amount of money is not the same in all price categories. The equation should be written as follows:(3)

$$M^* V^* = p_1 q_1 + p_2 q_2 + p_3 q_3 + \cdots + p_n q_n$$

where n commodity groups can be distinguished(3).

b. The Quantity Theory

The oldest and best known explanation of the value of money and the changes in that value suffers from the weakness of the exchange equation. The two must not be confused, however: The exchange equation itself is neutral and says nothing of the causal relationship between the four components. The equation is to be considered as an identity, not as a behaviour relation—two concepts that are often confused.(4)

Since moderate price fluctuations appear possible without a rise in M^*, the theory can be valid only in the long term. Some supporters of the quantity theory, however, have devoted considerable attention to the effects of short-term fluctuations in the amount of money on economic activity.

Not only can the level of absolute prices be influenced, but also the relationship between the various prices (the relative prices), without altering the general level of prices. Stability, therefore, is not necessarily a guarantee of the neutrality of money (relative prices remain unchanged).

The relationship between M^* and P^* can, naturally, best be studied when V^* and T^* are constant. Particularly since 1930, however, it has been more common for an increase in M^* not to lead to a price rise, because V^* has decreased (hoarding). A fall in M^* usually does not lead to a price cut because of the rigidity of prices. In other words, the quantity theory seems to be applicable only in the case of full employment.

The direction of causality (M^* is the independent variable) is usually correct, but psychological factors and autonomous changes in profits and wages can cause a rise in P^* to bring about an increase in M^*. During periods of sharp price rises (e.g. in Germany after the two world wars) confidence in the currency is lost and there is a preference for goods rather than money. By this process prices are raised again, and this causes a further increase in M^*. Finally, there is also the possibility of indirect action (M^* influences interest rates and ultimately production costs and P^*).

4. THE CASH-BALANCE THEORY

This theory states that the quantity of money, M^*, is at any given moment equal to the aggregate of cash balances held by the economic units. (For a given *period,* the *average* quantity of money equals the aggregate of *average* cash balances.) These cash balances also represent a given share, b, of the total value of goods traded so that: $M^* = bP^*T^*$.

As was the case with the transactions equation of exchange, the cash-balance equation expresses an evident truth: The value of the supply of money is equal to the value of the goods for which purchasing power is retained in the form of money.

While in the transactions equation of exchange one pays attention exclusively to that portion of the amount of money destined for current transactions, in the cash-balance equation one pays attention mainly to that part retained for unforeseen expenditure. And V^* or b is different for each part – rather stable for the first but not for the second (under the influence of hoarding and dishoarding).

Stressing the connection between b and income actually fits in better with modern theory. The objections to the quantity theory, however, remain valid. The cash-balance theory is likewise a monetary approach to the explanation of the variations in economic life. For this purpose, both theories are based on the fluctuations, of M^*V^* and M^*/b respectively. In expenditure analysis, on the other hand, changes in economic activity are explained by means of consumption and investment decisions – that is, by the fluctuations of $C + I$ (but $C + I$ and M^*V^* are not equivalent: $C + I$ only consists of expenditure for finished products, whereas M^*V^* comprise all payments for production factors and semifinished products too and is therefore larger than $C + I$). Depending on the approach adopted, the government uses different instruments of economic policy: on the one hand monetary policy, and on the other, control of the circular flow.

The quantity theory and the cash-balance theory are too limited as general analytical tools, though they may provide useful indications. It must be remembered that the equations concerned 'are nothing more or less than shorthand expressions designed to indicate the nature of the variables whose operations can be shown to influence prices',[(5)] and that these variables have still to be thoroughly investigated. Psychological factors are of great importance here: 'It appears difficult to arrive at a full understanding of fluctuations in the value of money . . . without taking qualitative considerations and psychological analyses into account'.[(6)]

5. CONCLUSION

Once more, we must conclude that the theories considered give only partial explanations. Furthermore, there is not the slightest unanimity of opinion concerning the analysis of either the general level of income or that of prices.

7 THE THEORY OF ECONOMIC GROWTH

As a rule, economic growth is not measured against production capacity, which is very difficult to estimate, but against national production. In this chapter, we define economic growth as a sustained increase in the net real national product (or income) per inhabitant.

We shall examine the Harrod-Domar theory, the neoclassical theory and W. Rostow's theory. We shall also deal with the factors of economic growth. Furthermore, we shall ignore the question of whether economic growth is desirable in the long run. Some authors, indeed, are fundamentally against economic growth. The antropocentric—and unscientific—basis on which the theory of economic growth proceeds is, according to J.H. Culbertson, a consequence of the 'Judeo-Christian belief, the idea that the universe was built to serve man, as a means to his ultimate exaltation'.[(1)] According to the same author, earlier civilisations perished because of overpopulation and pollution.

1. THE HARROD-DOMAR THEORY

According to this theory,[(2)] the relative change in the national income (g) is determined by the ratio between the propensity to save (s) and the capital-output ratio (k) as follows: $g = s/k$.

Similar to the transactions equation of exchange, this formula gives the factors that are relevant to an analysis, but it tells us nothing about the factors themselves.

The theory is based on unrealistic assumptions. The capital-output ratio does not remain constant. Authors who consider it an acceptable working hypothesis to regard the capital-output ratio as constant, are relying on excessively limited material. Insofar as reliable data are available (the calculation of macroeconomic capital is quite a feat), the ratio (as well as changes in the ratio) differs from country to country. Special circumstances have repeatedly played a role. Technological progress is frequently embodied in the formation of capital, so that production is compared not only with capital but also with the technological progress embodied in capital goods. If this technological progress is not maintained, then the capital-output ratio will be too low in the next period. According to P. Streeten, 'the capital-output ratio can be of no assistance to the planner in deciding where, when, how and how much to invest'.[(3)]

Normally, a difference in growth between labour and capital provokes substitution phenomena. This substitution is considered impossible in the Harrod-Domar theory, where the growth rate of the national product is identical to that of the capital goods stock. This is more a short-term hypothesis rather than long term.

It is surprising that the Harrod-Domar theory does not try to show a link between an increase in the exogenously determined total or active population and the increase in the derived demand for labour that results from the increase in the stock of capital goods (labour and capital are assumed to be in a fixed ratio to each other).

A similar observation may be made about the propensity to save. Some authors, including N. Kaldor[(4)] and J. Robinson[(5)], think that, for instance, the propensity to save differs in the case of income from employment and income from entrepreneurship.

2. THE NEOCLASSICAL THEORY

Neoclassical theory assumes two production factors—perfect substitutability and flexible prices. It is also based on a constant propensity to save, but it does not assume a fixed capital-output ratio.

It must be again stressed that the propensity to save is not constant. Most prices and wages are rigid; to resume flexible prices is therefore unrealistic (unemployment is not absorbed when wages fall). The ratio between capital and labour has not been fixed once and for all, and perfect substitutability is not possible either. While the Harrod-Domar theory is a macroeconomic theory, the neoclassical theory is fundamentally microeconomic.

3. W. ROSTOW'S THEORY

Rostow's thesis[(6)] does not concur with the statistical material available. The process of growth and the trend of investment are gradual: They do not advance by fits and starts. The industrial 'revolution' in England 'was the cumulation of a four-century period of advance in techniques'.[(7)] It is not clear what criteria can be used in order to distinguish one stage from another. How the 'reactive nationalism', a characteristic of the takeoff, must be interpreted, is not clear. Nor is it possible to establish in advance what industries should provide the thrust to set off economic growth. While in most cases agricultural development precedes growth in the industrial sector, the two frequently go hand in hand.

Rostow's scheme fails to take into account the fact that the less-developed countries can now avail themselves of Western experts and up-to-date equipment and thus avoid not a little trial and error and misdirected investment. They experience difficulties in exporting, however, because competition having increased in the meantime importers expect higher standards of quality and lower prices than, for instance, at the beginning of the nineteenth century, when Britain was the only exporter on an international scale.

Rostow has the merit of not wanting to give a purely economic theory of economic growth. However, some of his statements concerning the link between economics and politics are at least susceptible to criticism (e.g. when he says that industrialism goes together with a strive for democracy).

4. THE FACTORS OF ECONOMIC GROWTH

Numerous growth theories, three of which havc already been dealt with, are based on very few (in most cases only one or two) determining elements.

Of the many factors that are of importance to economic growth, besides the institutional, political and social circumstances under which production takes place, particular mention must be made of population, natural resources, capital, education and technological progress.

a. Population

No connection exists between the growth rate of the national product and that of the population. Although demographic expansion can contribute to economic growth by inducing new investment, it acts rather as a brake when the growth of population does not give rise to an increase in demand. This is the case in most of the less-developed countries. The developed countries could provide material assistance in the efforts being made to introduce birth control in the less-developed countries: 'The modest contributions that rich countries might make to facilitate this crucial part of the modernization process could well count for more than all they are prepared to do in the realm of conventional aid'.[(8)]

b. Natural Conditions

It is difficult to generalize regarding the connection between soil conditions or mineral resources and economic growth. The possession of rich ore deposits is not a sufficient condition for economic development (a certain monopoly power is required, e.g. petrolcum), nor is the lack of them any hindrance (e.g. Japan): The extension of transport facilities, in particular, has incurred cheapness in the shipment of raw materials. Whereas in some countries with abundant natural resources the average national income shows little increase (e.g. Indonesia), countries not so well off in this respect have shown steady progress.

c. Capital

Economic growth generally accompanies an increase in the importance of industry (to the detriment of agriculture). Hence the industrialisation policy of less-developed countries. Theoretically, preference should be given to investment in as many industries as possible. There are many risks involved in capital investment in only one industry; income must also be raised elsewhere to absorb that industry's increased production. A big push is needed, then, to achieve balanced growth. In fact, balanced growth cannot be realized because there are insufficient financial means and a scarcity of entrepreneurs; and in some cases it would thwart the international division of labour. Some authors, including A.O. Hirschman,[9] even advocate deliberately unbalanced growth.

An increase in investment in the less-developed countries is only possible where there is efficient management and skilled labour – factors that are not normally available. Hence the importance of education and technical assistance. Here, however, a minimum of programming is required – as in the developed countries. For example, there are too many lawyers and too few engineers in the less-developed countries, and primary and secondary education are often neglected in favour of higher education, so that the number of university graduates exceeds the number of openings for them.

d. Education

I. Fisher[10] already pointed out that people were to be considered as 'human capital', and expenditure on education as investment in these people (A. Marshall did not agree).[11] Since T.W. Schultz defended this proposition in 1960,[(12)] many economists have been advocates of the 'human capital approach'.

Numerous, but not always reliable, calculations suggest that the rate of interest on human capital does not differ much from the interest on nonhuman capital. Apart from the difficulties involved in measuring the quality of human capital, the fact that education is not only an investment but also a consumption is overlooked. Not all education has economic purposes (e.g. history of art).

Furthermore, income is not solely determined by productivity (which is influenced by education). Although both education and scientific research are of importance to economic growth, it is difficult to establish a simple connection between the two factors and economic growth.

e. Technological Advance

According to R. Solow,[(13)] technological advance accounted for 85 percent of the growth in the American economy (national income per employee) between 1909 and 1945. E.F. Denison[(14)] quotes 62 percent for the United States in the period 1950–62 and 80 percent for Northwestern Europe (where the highest figure for any one country was 86 percent for Western Germany).

However, for the authors mentioned 'technological advance' is a broader concept. It is not a consequence of microeconomic innovation, but a macroeconomic residual factor. That part of the growth rate of the national product which cannot be explained by the increase in labour and capital is attributed to technological advance – not only technological advance in the strict sense but also improvement in the quality of production factors (e.g. a higher standard of education) and the way in which factors are combined to make for efficient production (e.g. more efficient management, economies of scale, external economies). The sum of these changes entails increased production per unit of input. Thus, the national income rises because there are changes in factor inputs and because output per unit of input increases (i.e. technological advance in the broader sense). It would be preferable to speak of production per unit of input to avoid confusion with technological advance proper.

Although the relevant literature is of recent date, a number of theories have been proclaimed concerning the role of technological advance in economic growth. R. Solow,[15] for instance, holds that technological advance is reflected in or is incorporated in the investment of the current year ('the latest vintage of capital'). Others remark that technological advance need not necessarily be embodied in labour or capital but should rather be considered a third production factor. K. Arrow[16] sees technological advance as a consequence rather than as a cause of economic growth.

In neoclassical theory, technological advance is considered an exogenous factor. This is a one-sided point of view: Technological advance may also be the result of expenditure on education or research, in which case it is of an endogenous character, and cannot be a residual factor. The rough estimates of this residual factor and its components (e.g. education, economies of scale) could just as well be replaced by other, quite different, estimates. The hypotheses (e.g. pure competition) on which the method is based are indeed very unrealistic. Technological advance has without question been important in economic growth, but it is impossible to ascertain exactly to what extent the one explains the other. Whether technological advance is capital saving or labour saving (or neutral) is again very difficult to say. (An innovation may be labour saving, but it may raise the relative wage level.)

5. CONCLUSION

Economic growth is a difficult and complicated matter. John H. Adler quite accurately points out that

> the experience of the postwar period shows the complexity and many-sidedness of the process of economic development, on the one hand, and how little we know and how much we still have to learn about it, on the other.[17]

It should not surprise us that 'we seem as far from a *general* theory as ever'.[18]

The significance of each growth factor differs from country to country—the institutional circumstances in particular. This applies especially to the less-developed countries. It is a fact that there are relatively few features common to the economies of these countries: small stock of capital goods and little technological knowhow, few good entrepreneurs or managers. And there are great differences in natural resources, institutional circumstances and population. It stands to reason that economic policy in a densely populated country (with substantial disguised unemployment) will differ from that in a thinly populated country.

A theory that will serve for one particular country or group of countries is not necessarily applicable to another. India, for instance, is often regarded (wrongly) as *the* example of a less-developed country. In view of this misconception, more attention is now paid to a classification of the different countries—with a theory for each type. There is no need to look for a special development theory for the less-developed countries. Attempts made along these lines have had few results. With the exception of W.W. Rostow's theory(19) we have been offered only partial explanations. The economic dualism assumed by some authors, for instance (coexistence of a relatively small, modern, capital-intensive sector and a traditional, mainly agricultural sector), can be found in developed countries too, though to a lesser extent.

All this explains the opinion of Sir John Hicks:

> No attempt is made to present a Theory of Economic Growth . . . which is to be defended as the theory, superior in every respect, or even in every important respect, to any other. I do not think that there is such a theory; I much doubt if there can be!(20)

8 THE THEORY OF INTERNATIONAL TRADE

In this chapter, we will discuss the theory of comparative cost, the Heckscher-Ohlin theory, the theory of purchasing-power parity and the modern theory of balance-of-payments equilibrium.

1. THE THEORY OF COMPARATIVE COST

According to this theory, it is not the absolute but the comparative cost (which depends solely on the input of labour) that constitutes the decisive factor in determining which goods are traded with other countries. Even if a country were able to manufacture everything more inexpensively than any other country, it would be to its advantage to concentrate on producing the most profitable commodities and leave the less profitable goods to other countries.

However, the assumptions under which the theory proceeds have no factual basis. For example, costs are not due to labour alone. Moreover, labour is not homogeneous (otherwise there could be no international differences in costs). Furthermore, there are transport costs, and the higher these costs, the less the advantage that divergent comparative costs will yield. In reality, calculations are not made with costs in kind, but with currency units. Therefore, the concept of 'opportunity cost', or 'substitution cost',[(1)] introduced by G. Haberler offers no solution, since here again, they are expressed in real units (i.e. the amount of the one commodity that has to be sacrificed in order to increase the production of another commodity by one unit).

While the theory tells us within what limits the exchange ratio must lie, it gives no indications as to the actual ratio, nor as to the quantities traded. This is because it disregards the importance of demand. At a later date, attempts were made—notably by J.S. Mill[(2)]—to take account of demand, but here too the initial assumptions were unrealistic.

Since it was from the theory of comparative cost that the need for international division of labour and free trade was derived, it was not surprising that protectionism was justified because certain hypotheses in the theory (e.g. full employment, constant costs) were inconsistent with the hard facts.

Comparative costs, moreover, do not account per se for the development of trade: They themselves have to be explained.

Speaking of the classical theory, J. Viner accurately states his own conviction that . . . 'it would be a mistake to carry its rehabilitation so far as to claim for it, even in its improved and modernized form, adequacy as a theory to guide policy in the present-day world'.[(3)] And he continues with the often quoted passage:

> The world has changed greatly, and is now a world of planned economies, of state trading, of substantially arbitrary and inflexible national price structures, and of managed instability in exchange rates. The classical theory is not directly relevant for such a world, and it may be that for such a world there is and can be no relevant *general* theory'.[(4)]

The multiplicity of factors that may affect import and export prices, 'cannot be reduced to a *meaningful* simple formula',[(5)] and E.E. Hagen is right in claiming that '. . . there is no general basis for determining what a country's comparative advantage will be. One must simply look, to see what it is'.[(6)]

2. THE HECKSCHER-OHLIN THEORY

The basis now used is not one, but several factors of production. The production functions are assumed to be the same in every country: The same combination of factors of production yields the same production. The factor combination differs from product to product (e.g. production of textiles is more labour-intensive than that of cars). Hence, the various goods produced in a given country can be ranked according to their capital-intensiveness (or labour-intensiveness): this classification is assumed to be constant and is not influenced by alterations in the relative factor prices. (This is an unrealistic hypothesis.) In other words, factor-intensity reversal (so that textiles are produced more capital-intensively than cars) does not occur. In addition, reasoning is not in real terms but in terms of money costs. The other hypotheses in the classical theory, however, have been adopted (such as constant returns and pure competition).

Under these conditions, differences in comparative costs are due to varying factor price ratios. The latter are determined by the quantity and quality of the manpower, capital goods and raw materials available in the various regions, and also by climatological conditions and the state of the soil. If labour (capital) is the relatively abundant and consequently cheap factor, a comparative advantage is obtained in the production and exportation of relatively labour-intensive (capital-intensive) goods.

Analysis on the basis of two or more factors is certainly more realistic, but the difficulties persist: These factors are not homogeneous.

Production techniques are not the same everywhere. Many goods can be produced, either capital-intensively or labour-intensively, at the same cost. As stated previously, the assumption that factor-intensity reversal cannot occur does not hold well in practice.

More than half the volume of international trade is between countries with roughly the same factor ratios. For this, the Heckscher-Ohlin theory can provide no explanation. Nor, since the factor endowments are assumed to be unchanged, can it account for substantial short-term changes in the pattern of trade. In the longer term, however, trade has an effect on factors: Instead of factor distribution accounting for the pattern of international trade, it is the latter that may give an idea of the former. (Trade, for instance, causes migration because of higher demand for labour in certain areas.

Owing to government action (e.g. the fixing of minimum wages and social legislation), factor prices do not necessarily reflect the scarcity differences. For that matter, such scarcity differences are not always accorded the attention they deserve. For prestige reasons, preference is sometimes given to capital-intensive production where labour-intensive production is actually called for.

Although Ohlin's theory undoubtedly has an element of truth, it is clear from the foregoing that it is '. . . somewhat vague and conditional'.(7) G. Haberler too stresses that:

> . . . with many factors of production, some of which are qualitatively incommensurable as between different countries, and with dissimilar production functions in different countries, no sweeping *a priori* generalizations concerning the composition of trade are possible'.(8)

S. Mookerjee concludes a study devoted to the Heckscher-Ohlin theory in the same way: 'In general . . . no definite *a priori* generalization concerning the composition of trade is possible'.(9)

3. TRADE AND ECONOMIC GROWTH

There are also contradictory views concerning the influence of foreign trade on growth. According to some of these views, an expansion of exports is a prerequisite for economic development; according to others, it exercises an adverse influence. Whichever standpoint is adopted, the effect on economic policy is significant: in the one case, growth is to be secured by expanding exports; in the other, by import substitution.

Those authors who regard trade as a favourable growth factor—notably Mill, Marshall, Viner, Haberler—point to the beneficial feedbacks, by which trade gives an impetus to growth: It widens the market, thus opening up the way for improved production processes (economies of large-scale production, improvements in technology) and curbs domestic monopolies. Many countries, moreover, are too small to pursue an intense industrialisation policy.

Especially since the Second World War, however, many authors have shown trade pessimism, at least with respect to less-developed countries. H.W. Singer[10] and G. Myrdal[11] hold extreme views on the subject. From the export-oriented enclaves in the less-developed countries, their argument runs, there are relatively few spill-overs (or spread effects) to the rest of the economy, so that dual societies are created or reinforced, while other industries and values may be destroyed (backwash effects). Trade does not contribute to the raising of the less-developed countries' living standards.

After pointing out that the economic growth of the 'new' states which sprang up in the past century – the United States, Canada, Argentina and Australia – was attributable to the substantial expansion of West-European, and especially British demand for foodstuffs and raw materials, Ragnar Nurkse[12] goes on to assert that the less-developed countries are no longer confronted with such an increasing demand (cf. the rise of synthetics) and that foreign trade, contrary to what happened in the last century, cannot be a prime mover of growth.

It has been stressed[13] that external demand is not necessarily the dominant factor in economic growth, which in the first place depends on internal structural or supply factors, and it is often these factors that account for the lag in exports suffered by the less-developed countries (for instance, population growth). Nor can it be argued that no effect has been exerted on the rest of the economy by these enclaves.[14] I.B. Kravis[15] shows that Nurkse's observations concerning exports do not hold for the nineteenth and twentieth centuries; during the nineteenth century, both the United States and Australia showed few signs of export-led growth; countries with a low growth rate, such as India and Ceylon, achieved an export expansion similar to that of the United States and Canada. In the twentieth century, less-developed countries have even greater trade opportunities. If the proportion of exports accounted for by the less-developed countries as a group has declined, this can be explained by the fact that they:

> . . . have not on the whole taken full advantage of world trade opportunities, often incorrectly attributing their difficulties to unfavourable external conditions when the most important problems have been at home'.[16]

Exports can stimulate growth (as in the case of Britain from 1780 to 1800 and from 1850 to 1870). The rapid progress achieved by the Japanese economy is also usually attributed to export expansion.

It is noteworthy that for the past ten years or so the less-developed countries have attached more importance to their export potential. In UNCTAD (United Nations Conference on Trade and Development) publications, too, attention is drawn to the '. . . dominant role in stimulating . . . overall economic growth . . .'[17] of exports. Emphasis is placed on the fact that a better growth rate '. . . will depend on the expansion of demand in developed market economies and in the socialist countries at rates substantially above the average achieved in the last decade . . .',[18], but little mention is made of the fact that in many cases domestic supply conditions should be improved. As long as '. . . sufficient social and political change, as well as economic change . . .' has not been brought about '. . . to make the economy more responsive to the stimulus from trade . . .',[19] there is little point in stimulating exports. Hence, according to H. Myint, it is '. . . paradoxical to describe export expansion policies as "outward-looking" when their success vitally depends on domestic economic policies . . .'.[20]

There is now more or less a consensus that no general pronouncements can be made on the relationship between trade and growth. Whether international trade is advantageous, neutral or injurious depends on a multiplicity of factors, including natural resource endowment, the kind of economic ownership (foreign or domestic) in the export sector, and the type of economic policy pursued. Whether an outward-looking or an inward-looking policy is preferable must not be determined by ideological considerations, but by the extent to which each policy, through the mobilisation of domestic production factors and the development of a different attitude, contributes to economic development. Moreover, the necessity of '. . . a case-by-case approach, tailoring policies to individual country situations . . .'[21] is being—as previously stressed—recognised more and more.

4. THE THEORY OF PURCHASING-POWER PARITY

The theory of purchasing-power parity, which was expounded in a modern formulation by Gustav Cassel after 1918,[22] states that the exchange rate or external value of a currency is determined by the domestic value or purchasing-power parity of the foreign currencies concerned (in case of fixed exchange rates, how the purchasing power or price levels are determined).

In the comparative version of the purchasing-power-parity theory, changes in purchasing power are analysed in relation to a specific reference period. However, it is difficult to find a reference period that is marked by a genuine equilibrium of exchange rates. We ought really to go back to pre-1914 days, but in the meantime every country's economic structure has changed.

The choice of indices is not easy.[(23)] Prices of many world-market products (e.g. commodities) show only slight differences on national markets, with the result that the corresponding index numbers prove to be of little use. More reliance is therefore to be placed on domestic-price indices (retail prices, wages, cost of living). If the cost-of-living index has risen more in one country than in another with a simultaneous wage increase, the adverse effects of these movements are experienced by costs and selling prices.

The price level is not always the decisive factor in the volume of imports and exports. A change in demand for certain commodities, such as that which may result from inventions (e.g. sodium nitrate and artificial fertilizer), may cause a disturbance of the balance-of-payments equilibrium without any alteration of the purchasing-power parity. Modifications of customs tariffs frequently have similar consequences.

The purchasing-power parity relates to only a part of the balance of payments. Capital movements are not taken into consideration (e.g. imports of securities). Cassel himself has pointed out that, apart from the purchasing-power parity, a great many other factors exercise an influence on exchange rates.

Many countries' currencies are indeed linked to that of another economically strong country. In such cases the exchange rate does not hinge on the purchasing-power parity, but the purchasing power of one currency is conditioned by that of another currency and the exchange rate between them.

5. THE THEORY OF BALANCE-OF-PAYMENTS EQUILIBRIUM

The modern theory relates restoration of equilibrium more closely to the fluctuations in employment and the national income than was the case of the gold standard system. This theory applies only when there is no full employment (constant prices). It is based on the assumptions that the marginal propensities to save and to import remain constant and that it is always possible to finance deficits, which in point of fact is not so. It further postulates that exports result from current production (and not from stocks). In the less-developed countries, import requirements are becoming so heavy (demonstration effect) that the theory cannot be applied to these areas.

Like the classical doctrine, this theory is based on an automatically operating mechanism, but the balance of payments is not necessarily brought into equilibrium in the modern theory. Instead of price fluctuations, it is mainly variations in the level of employment and the national income that perform a regulatory function. In fact, both income and price fluctuations play a role, but their importance varies from country to country.

Yet every country at least tries to maintain stability in the national income, employment and prices and therefore endeavours to counteract such oscillations. It does not acquiesce in an equilibrium rate of exchange that has large-scale unemployment as its concomitant. Such a policy contributes to the uncertainty surrounding an automatic correction of the balance of payments.

6. CONCLUSION

From the foregoing it is obvious that neither the theory of comparative cost nor the Heckscher-Ohlin theory can really be called satisfactory. H.W.J. Wijnholds justifiably believes that 'too much time has been wasted already in patching up a theory (of comparative cost) that is faulty in its very foundations'.[24] To conceal its drawbacks, the theory of comparative cost is sometimes formulated so vaguely (for instance, the 'law' of comparative prices) that it is certainly not capable of explaining the true situation.

The fact is that an explanation is sought for differences in prices, as the decisions made by importers and exporters are based on them. The theory of comparative cost assumes that prices in international exchange are a reflection of comparative costs. This implies, in particular, that the price system operates in a highly flexible manner (pure competition), that exchange rates are selected appropriately and that there are no barriers to trade (which, as already pointed out, are unrealistic hypotheses). In many cases, international division of labour can only be accounted for by historical or political circumstances. International restrictive agreements frequently influence international trade. The Heckscher-Ohlin theory is somewhat applicable to natural resources, but the influence of this factor is steadily declining as a result of the downward trend of transport costs.

There is no simple explanation for international trade because of the multiplicity of factors that may affect import and export prices (e.g. the importance of the domestic market and the technological lead).

Despite the foregoing objections and its limited applicability, the theory of purchasing-power parity may, in some circumstances, yield concrete data. In this respect, the theory of balance-of-payments equilibrium is disappointing.

9 THE LIMITED PRACTICABILITY OF THE THEORY

In this chapter, we will discuss some limiting factors of economic theory.

1. ISOLATION FROM OTHER SCIENCES

From the preceding chapters we see that economics develops in marked isolation from the other sciences. In economics, there is little reference to results of recent research in, for instance, sociology, psychology, history and politicology. 'The contemporary economist is less of a jurist, less of a historian, less of a sociologist, less of a philosopher and less of an honest man than his predecessors. For him, economics is sufficient'.[(1)] However, economic phenomena cannot be understood without a knowledge of the political and social circumstances under which they take place. W. Sombart even argued that 'any economic theory is ultimately sociology'.[(2)] J.M. Keynes, like many economists before him,[(3)] has stressed that the 'Master

Economist' must, to a certain degree, be a mathematician, a historian, a politician and a philosopher.[(4)] A. Gray[(5)] believes that when he is merely an economist, 'he is damned'. G. L. S. Shackle chimes in with the assertion that to be a complete economist:

> a man needs only to be a mathematician, a philosopher, a psychologist, an anthropologist, a historian, a geographer, and a student of politics; a master of prose exposition; and a man of the world with experience of practical business and finance, and understanding of the problems of administration, and a good knowledge of four or five foreign languages. All this in addition, of course, to familiarity with the economic literature itself.[(6)]

He adds that 'the good economist must be like a bottle of wine . . . he must mature'. If a 'complete economist' does not exist, every economist must nevertheless attempt to acquire a minimum knowledge of the related sciences.[(7)] Indeed:

> if the economist is not willing to study (certain political and social conditions), alone or together with the representatives of the other disciplines, he must renounce explaining economic phenomena, and give up advising in matters of political economy, except within very narrow limits[(8)]

and K. Boulding goes even further: 'I have been gradually coming under the conviction, disturbing for a professional theorist, that there is no such thing as economics – there is only social science applied to economic problems'.[(9)] In fact, E. Malinvaud complains about 'the lack of proper theories for dealing with the interactions between economic and social developments'.[(10)]

For instance, expatiating on the role of trade unions is pointless without involving political and social considerations; the same applies to discoursing upon consumers' decisions without bringing in psychology.

From the preceding discussion, it does not follow that economic theory did not progress as far as other social sciences. Sociology even deteriorates and sociological 'theory' seems to be limited to the setting up and commenting upon surveys. Moreover, sociology and especially political science often rely on economics. Consequently, it would be unwise to entertain too many illusions regarding closer cooperation with other sciences, the latter being in the grip of an even greater crisis situation than economics.

2. UNREALISTIC HYPOTHESES

Far too often, the theories we have studied proceed from unrealistic hypotheses. These include perfect competition, divisibility and substitutability of production factors, homogeneous goods, mobility of production factors and profit maximization. Equally reprehensible is the simplistic device of explaining economic phenomena by only one production factor (e.g. the Harrod-Domar theory). Even an analysis based on three production factors is scarcely an acceptable simplification. There are countless subdivisions of both skilled and unskilled labour. Capital goods, too, take various forms. Factor endowments vary from country to country and are unevenly spread. 'Economic models unrelated to reality are constructed, criticized, amended, on occasion commended and then alas, completely forgotten' complains J. Galbraith.(11) This is echoed by C.M. Cyert and C.L. Hedrick: 'The real world still escapes our models'.(12)

Nor can the marginalism that goes along with perfect competition account for the prices of goods, services and production factors. The concepts involved, such as marginal revenue, marginal product and marginal costs, cannot be calculated and for the most part they are actually unknown.

What happens, in fact, is that an unrealistic economic structure (assuming such a structure ever existed) is to some extent used as a basis.

To assume that all phenomena involved in the argumentation are constant is dangerous: the *ceteris paribus* clause is a 'very tricky assumption'(13) and a 'slippery tool'.(14)

a. Testing and Falsifying

It is not enough to accept that hypotheses conform with reality – they need to be tested as well.(15) One can generally find observations to support a theory. If observations are consistent with the theory – and the hypotheses underlying a theory must be stated in such a way that they can be collated with the facts – this is still no proof that the theory is right. One can only prove that it is *not* right and therefore one must examine if the hypotheses have been falsified. According to K.R. Popper, theories that are not falsifiable belong to metaphysics, and not to an empirical science.(16) Thus, the assertion that a particular constitution cannot be maintained in the long run is not falsifiable, because no time limit is specified.(17)

After rejecting certain hypotheses, one must formulate others and ascertain whether they, too, are falsifiable. The progress of science depends on the interaction between the formulation of hypotheses and their rejection. T. Kuhn(18) does not entirely agree with the view that theories are constantly being adapted to the lessons of experience: At a certain moment in time, he claims, a theory is replaced by another, giving a better explanation. We see only a difference in degree between the two standpoints: In many cases they coincide.

b. Nonoperational Concepts

In this connection, the large number of nonoperational concepts in economics is to be deplored. Why concepts such as 'demand' and 'supply' are used, is a mystery. In reality, they cannot be quantified. In economic analysis other concepts, which to a certain extent are determinable, are assumed to be constant (e.g. the marginal propensity to save, to consume and to import and technological knowledge in input-output analysis), whereas in point of fact, they sometimes fluctuate considerably. F. Machlup concludes a survey of the relevant problems as follows: '. . . while there are important numerical constants in the natural sciences, there are none in the social sciences'.(19)

3. MATHEMATIZATION OF ECONOMICS

Economists often select the hypotheses on which to base their theories and models according to whether they can be represented by a preferably highly complex mathematical formula or graph. They operate from purely deductive principles (thinking they can proceed as would a mathematician or a physician).

Now mathematics can be a useful tool in stating economic problems, but today it is becoming an end in itself for some people –

so much so that the 'nonmathematical practitioner is laboring under a dark suspicion (despite the history of economic thought) that nothing he does will be worthwhile'.[20] Much more than in 1932, when J. Robinson made the point, 'the subject matter of economics is neither more nor less than its own technique',[21] and we agree with L. Robbins when he says that:

> For all the proliferation of diagrams in recent literature, I doubt whether, analytically, we have advanced very far beyond Marshall's few lines of algebra; and I suspect that, in practical judgment and sense of proportion, we are often some way behind'.[22]

A. Marshall himself formulated (not without humour) the following rules for the use of mathematics:

1. Use mathematics as a shorthand language, rather than as an engine of inquiry.
2. Keep to them till you have done.
3. Translate into English.
4. Then illustrate by examples that are important in real life.
5. Burn the mathematics.
6. If you can't succeed in 4, burn 3. This last I did often.[23]

In the same year as Robbins, F.D. Graham complained:

> All the inconvenient freight of fact has been discarded by the more recondite practitioners until the "science" has come to move in a realm of pure abstraction useful for purposes of cerebration but of steadily declining practical importance'.[24]

Mathematical stylishness is preferred to convenience of calculation. Not the slightest thought is given to communicating with other economists, let alone with the intelligent layman.[25]

From the foregoing it follows that:

> the economists, and especially the econometrists, do not hesitate to launch new models on the scientific market without ascertaining empirically whether the new models are to be preferred to the old ones. In this way, the number of models increases rapidly, they become an encumbrance and contradict each other and they breed distrust and scepticism.[26]

'Economics has become a monstrous battlefield covered with ruins of models'–says E. Böhler–'on each of which sits one economist in sublime solitude'.(27) Hence the following complaints: 'The whole economics profession . . . is an example of that monumental misallocation of intellectual resources which is one of the most striking phenomena of our time'.(28) 'What is needed is a reallocation of economic brainpower towards the analysis and interpretation of the real world'.(29)

E.J. Mishan has given us a witty but accurate description of this kind of sport, and we cannot resist the temptation to reproduce it in full–with the permission of the author.

> To glance through the journals of the last ten or twenty years is to lose oneself in a carnival of possibility theorems. With so few empirical checks to speculative fervour the opportunities for economic science-fiction are practically boundless. One has only to outline the familiar routine of theory and counter-theory in economics to recognise, rather ruefully, the nature of the intellectual rake's progress involved. Thus, a well-known theory has it that, if we assume propositions *A, B,* and *C,* it can be shown that if *P then Q,* and *if R then S.* Some seminal mind now challenges this theory; to wit, if instead of *B* we assume B^*, and instead of *C* we assume C^*, we have the paradoxical result that *if P then S,* and *if R then Q.* It will not be long before it is pointed out that in the long run B^* tends to *B* and that C^* tends to *C,* at least if we make the reasonable assumption of *E.* A further contribution will reveal that if we introduce a new relationship, *G,* it no longer follows that *if P then Q,* and it will be concluded therefore that the original model has made the tacit assumption of non-*G.* This new contribution will therefore be regarded as a more general theory on the grounds that non-*G* is but the limiting case of *G.*
>
> In the same spirit another paper will introduce a further relationship *H* and conclude that all non-*H* models are special cases only. A controversy then begins about whether the proposition *H* is consistent with the *A* postulate: certainly it is not if we admit a fairly common assumption *F.* A new article now points out that the *A* postulate has been misunderstood; it has been misinterpreted as A'. In reply to this discovery, it will be insisted that A' is the proper interpretation. Generality of approach is promoted in a taxonomic paper that deduces the implications of *A,* of A', and of both *A* and A' together. Someone writing for *Econometrica* will then juxtapose all the possibilities in matrix notation: depending on the conditions assumed the key variables can move in any direction. Somewhere else a literary digest of the controversy will be given and a new approach indicated. And so, notwithstanding occasional perorations of the what-we-need-is-some-systematic-empirical-investigation sort, the game goes on without respite. Economics

has become the thing that economists write about, and as such it has become the science of infinite conjecture.[30]

4. CONCLUSION

We need not be surprised that there are complaints about the inapplicability of the theory: '. . . a major portion of our current articles are not useful for decisions—nor are they likely to form a base upon which future knowledge to improve decisions can be built'.[31] This grievance concerning monetary problems is valid for the entire field of economics. Some authors even wonder whether they have done a useful job.[32] If people were to ask themselves this question in advance, perhaps there would be less useless literature published. Of course, one can maintain with M. Friedman that the (empirical) unrealism of the theory 'itself', or of its 'assumptions', is quite irrelevant to its validity and worth,[33] but then—we repeat—we must recognise that what we are engaged in is art for art's sake.

10 THE SIGNIFICANCE OF ECONOMIC THEORY

Now that we have stressed the limited practicability of economic theory, it is appropriate to examine what significance it still has. First we will discuss the aspects of determinism and predictability.

1. DETERMINISM

Many authors do not accept economic phenomena as being determined. According to P. Hennipman, this is wrong; the determinism of phenomena really implies that 'they are subject to certain laws, known or unknown'.[(1)] Sensu stricto, facts are only explained from known laws. The fact that phenomena are determined or determinable is – still according to P. Hennipman – not to be confused with logical determinism of theoretical solutions or, in other words, with the logical determinism that occurs, if it is proved that the economic variable to be explained from variables of a theoretical model has a unique value. Mathematically speaking, the equality of the number of unknowns and the number of independent equations is a necessary but not a sufficient condition. Economic theory tries to find such determined solutions.

P. Hennipman explains why determinism founded on facts (empirical) and theoretical (logical) determinism do not necessarily coincide; in theoretical models:

a. Only the most important explanatory variables are considered (to prevent confusion). There remains an 'inexplicable residue one might call the marginal indeterminedness of phenomena'.[2]
b. The diversity of historic conditions that accompany phenomena is overlooked; the determined variables are different in every situation. ('Structural indeterminedness of facts' is the expression employed.)
c. No quantitative empirical results are obtained; it is not necessarily assumed that facts are available.

One must, however, take into consideration the fact that the 'policy-maker' is only interested in empirical determinism, which is non-existent. In this connection we will deal with predictability.

2. PREDICTABILITY

In a sense, many economic statements are predictions: When in theory it is said that an increase in supply in a certain market, provided all other circumstances remain unchanged, leads to a drop in prices, one is predicting. When one speaks of predicting in economics, what one really means is assertions in connection with the course of, for instance, national income or the price level in the coming months or years.

The meagre balance of economics concerning these concrete predictions (in contrast with the theoretical, conditional predictions) is a fact. It is easy to compile extensive anthologies on erroneous predictions[3] of both national and international institutions, such as the European Economic Community, the European Coal and Steel Community, the Organisation for Economic Cooperation and Development. The phenomenon is not a new one. One need only point to experience obtained with the Harvard indicator. In Germany, it was predicted in 1933 that consumption of electricity in 1960 would amount to 32,000 million kWh. For the Federal Republic alone, consumption totalled 120,600 million kWh.[(4)]

From the empirical undeterminism of economic phenomena, it follows that making predictions is, if not impossible, at least very difficult; economic units do not necessarily maximize: Their reactions are unpredictable,[(5)] and furthermore, predictions sometimes influence the consumers' and producers' behaviour. It is too often assumed that many factors remain constant: If, for instance, the input-output table is used as an instrument of prediction, a proportional relation between inputs and outputs is assumed (technological knowledge remaining the same). This is scarcely a realistic hypothesis. That no influence is exerted by prices on the technological coefficients (as is implicitly assumed) is also improbable.

The specialized institutes – and there are hundreds of them in the world – whose predictions are based on extensive models do not achieve any better results. They 'are always one inflation too late in specifying the exact form of the price forecasting equations'.[(6)] Generally speaking, even in the best institutions the data obtained are very often changed arbitrarily, being based on 'feeling'. There are too many psychological and political variables (which influence the anticipations of the economic units) to insert them all in the models. D.B.J Schouten correctly believes that

> . . . any forecast concerning the pattern of the business cycle has only a limited value. Even the best-equipped cyclical-research bureau is unable at the present time to construct a reliable business-cycle prognosis for any longer period than a year.[(7)]

I do not believe predicting to be part of economic science's task: It already has its hands full describing and explaining economic phenomena. Hence, to condemn economics because of its failure to predict – as S. Schoeffler does[(8)] – cannot be upheld.

This view does not imply that the economist should not make predictions: However, the economist must state explicitly the large number of (unrealistic) hypotheses on which the predictions – in most cases extrapolations – are based.

The fact that predicting is considered part of the task of economics sometimes influences the formulation of assumptions. Thus, Milton Friedman thinks that 'the only relevant test of *validity* of a hypothesis is comparison of its predictions with experience';[9] in other words:

> . . . the relevant question to ask about 'assumptions' of a theory is not whether they are descriptively 'realistic', for they never are, but whether they are sufficiently good approximations for the purpose at hand. And this question can be answered only by seeing whether the theory works, which means whether it yields sufficiently accurate predictions.[10]

Friedman incorrectly believes that every abstraction assumes the use of false assumptions;[11] he does not, however, explain why the difference between assumptions and reality is of no importance.[12] If Friedman's point of view is accepted, practically any theory could be formulated (falsifying the assumptions being impossible; moreover, the theory must be consistent). Finally, the prediction itself is not explained. W. Leontief argues that 'The prevalence of such a point of view is, to a large extent, responsible for the state of splendid isolation in which our discipline nowadays finds itself'.[13]

3. THEORY OR METHOD?

Economic life is so complex and varied that the theory cannot take into account all the data available. It is obliged to simplify – to assume, for instance, that many factors remain constant (the *ceteris paribus* clause). The more we try to reduce it to a meaningful pattern, the less we succeed in truly reflecting the real world. Nevertheless, many economists are 'totally unconscious that their reasonings cannot, at one and the same time, be rigorous and yet capable of seizing all the essentials of reality'.[14] Hence, H.G. Johnson's view that 'if economic theory is to be applied to problems of economic policy this can most usefully be done within the context of a particular problem occurring in a particular environment'.[15] If we take simplification too far, he adds, theory can be more of a hindrance than a help. R. Triffin, too, points out that economic science, conceived otherwise:

> disencumbered, . . . of all the . . . limitations and taboos implied in the classical assumptions . . . will recognize the richness and variety of all concrete cases, and tackle each problem with due respect for its individual aspects.(16)

However much we may regret it, the fact remains that economics is of little empirical consequence. In a sense, economics is, to quote yet again the somewhat overstated view of Lord Keynes, 'a method rather than a doctrine, an apparatus of the mind, a technique of thinking'.(17)

4. CONCLUSION

It may be objected that the occasionally sharp criticism we have levelled against various concepts and theories in this contribution has been purely negative (since we have offered nothing as a substitute). This is to some extent true. However, it is no reason for continuing to uphold theories that are untenable. Furthermore, if we proceed from what has been said above we may doubt whether there *is* any substitute, whether a *general* economic theory is at all possible.

> It is in no way impossible that the difficulties encountered time and again by economic analysis are inherent in the subject matter of economics, that perfect solutions are out of reach, and that there is no method which can supply the certainty which is so often required from economics. But even if this is so, there is no cause for casting serious doubts on its significance and future.(18)

At any rate, the self-assurance evident in many publications and statements by economists often seems misplaced to us.

> The self-assurance accruing to any profession handling its subject mathematically has overtaken economists. With feelings of great confidence in this 'scientific' approach, they have developed a compensating distrust, indifference, if not disdain, towards the findings obtained by non-mathematical methods in other sciences.(19)

The layman is given the impression that economics is capable of solving all problems. Many economists simply will not admit that in many cases there just is no precise answer. What J. Tinbergen says with reference to the optimum savings' function:

> If is characteristic of the underdeveloped state of our science that virtually nothing empirical is known about this generalization and that, as a consequence, nothing sensible can be said about the optimum level of savings at present[20]

holds well, as our contribution will have shown, not only for this concept. We do not deny that economic science has advanced over the last twenty or thirty years, but the advice presented by F. Simiand in 1937 still applies: 'What economic science should be working on at the moment is realizing how very little it knows. This is perhaps the step forward that would do it most good'.[21]

Defeatism? No, realism:

> Even when it is not possible to give a complete explanation of the phenomena, to find all-embracing exact laws or to attain omniscience, thorough theoretical and empirical research is never pointless. A classification of possibilities, an orderly arrangement of the most important elements, the identification of important relations may, even when they do not solve all questions, increase perception sufficiently to be useful in practice. Knowing something is always better than knowing nothing.[22]

Besides, even 'in its present state (the science of economics yields) a considerable number of viewpoints which are of great scientific and practical value'.[23]

APPENDIX: ECONOMIC DOCTRINES

A survey of economic doctrines, or of economic ideas, must not be confused with economic history, which relates to economic facts—in other words, history studied from the standpoint of economics. Although communication and knowledge of facts is sometimes indispensable for ideas to be understood—they interact upon each other—it is best not to mingle the two concepts. The history of economic ideas cannot easily be divorced from the history of ideas in general.

This appendix is divided up according to major periods or schools, which in many cases overlap chronologically. Some authors have a place of their own. Each school forms both a continuation of and a reaction to the previous one.

1. ANCIENT AND MEDIEVAL TIMES

The Greeks, who were first and foremost politicians, never thought in purely economic terms; and, their manual labour was done for them by slaves. Even so, dissertations on money and interest are to be found in the works of Plato (427–347 BC) and Aristotle (384–322 BC).

Nor did the Romans devote much attention to economic problems. Only the agrarian question was examined, from a technical standpoint, by one or two authors.

Although labour became more respectable during the Middle Ages and was no longer done by slaves, the Church condemned any unrestrained craving for wealth. The development of trade prompted the clergy, the intellectuals of the time, to deliver judgments on economic questions. In these they invariably adopted an ethical standpoint. Thomas Aquinas (1226–74) defined the position of the Church towards the economic problems of the day: Interest was prohibited (time was God's and not marketable), whereas a compensation for the use of land was permissible. This was not regarded as exploitation but as a return for the natural properties of the soil made available. Later on, a moderate interest was allowed to be charged in respect of loans for non-consumption purposes which involved the lender in disadvantages (*damnum emergens*) or elimination of benefits (*lucrum cessans*). The price could only be a reward for the labour (*justum pretium*).

Also noteworthy for his monetary theory is Nicolas Oresme (1330–82). He was a proponent of a fixed relationship between the value of gold and that of silver, and he condemned the currency depreciation that prevailed in his day.

2. MERCANTILISM

The setting-up of nation states and the discovery of America (1492) had profound economic repercussions. The rationalist spirit gained more and more ground; profit-seeking assumed unusually large proportions. The formation of national armies made vast monetary demands on the sovereign rulers. The influence of the state increased at the expense of the authority of the Church.

a. Definition

The entire body of measures designed to make the state as powerful and as rich as possible was called the mercantilist system. The principal means employed to fulfil this aim were acquisition of a maximum amount of precious metals and the pursuance of an active population policy. Mercantilism – a name given by the physiocrats and adopted by Adam Smith – embodied that states possessing gold and silver (e.g. Spain) endeavoured to keep such metals in their possession, exports being prohibited. Other countries exerted every effort to obtain gold and silver; if they had no mines to develop, they had to stimulate imports of precious metals. This could only be done if there was a favourable trade balance.

The achievement of a surplus on trade was deemed to necessitate protectionism (organization and protection of trade and industry) which mainly assumed a maritime and colonial form (trade using the nation's own ships). Since it was impossible for all nations to accomplish these aims, a spirit of hostility developed among them out of necessity.

The mercantilists regarded interest as the price of money; they found that an increase in the quantity of money brought about a decline in interest rates. This view, which the classical authors contested, was later restored to favour by J.M. Keynes.

b. Forms

Mercantilism persisted as an economic system from about 1450 to 1750. Considering the length of this period and the number of countries with differing economic structures which conducted a mercantilist policy, it is not surprising that such a policy assumed a variety of forms, as described below.

Bullionism was a system which consisted in vigorous defence of stocks of precious metals, in particular by control over trade agreements and the prohibition of exports of such metals.

Industrialism (Colbertism) aimed at making the country rich by developing big 'manufactures'. The result, however, was a neglect of agriculture. Writers on the subject include Jean Antoine Bodin (1530–96), known for his naive quantity theory (he came to the conclusion that the cause of the rise in prices at that time – they trebled between 1500 and 1550 – was traceable to the excessive quantity of gold and silver coin, and gave as an additional reason coin-clipping by monarchs); and Antoine de Montchrétien (1576–1621), in whose *Traité de l'économie politique* the designation 'political economy' was used for the first time in 1616. While Bodin and de Montchrétien were also alive to commercial interests, the orthodox champion of industrialism was Jean-Baptiste Colbert (1619–83).

Commercial mercantilism focused attention mainly on methods of achieving a favourable trade balance. It was marked by a less protectionist attitude. Among its advocates were Thomas Mun (1571–1641), who considered the ban on gold exports a mistake because goods bought with gold could be exported at a profit after processing, Sir William Petty (1623–87), Josiah Child (1639–90) and Gregory King (1648–1712; cf. King's law). Richard Cantillon (ca. 1680–1734) was an economist with many ideas which put him ahead of his time.

Although the three tendencies described above were sometimes found simultaneously in one and the same country, in France it was mainly industrial, in the United Kingdom commercial, and in Germany and Spain metallic mercantilism that secured the most adherents. (In Germany it was also called Cameralism.)

According to John Law (1671–1729), money need not consist of coin, and paper money was even better. The term used for this concept is fiduciary mercantilism or neomercantilism.

Appraisal. The mercantilists had a one-sided view of wealth. The importance of money was overestimated. Even so, an increase in the quantity of money was necessary at times in order to counteract barter, which was induced by the lack of currency. Hence, self-centred international trade policies developed, often producing adverse consequences. The bullionist policy upheld by Spain was especially pernicious.

Numerous objections were subsequently raised to mercantilism. In the circumstances then prevailing, a great many measures were characterized by a high degree of realism. The anxiety concerning the demographic trend, for instance, was understandable after long-drawn-out wars had caused the population to drop considerably.

The economic problem was viewed in a national context – a transition from local to national economy.

3. PHYSIOCRACY

The physiocrats reacted against Colbertism and were therefore opposed to state intervention and to neglect of agriculture. They called themselves the *philosophes économistes* and during the years 1764–70 formed a sort of political party or sect. The leader of the school was François Quesnay (1694–1774), who studied medicine fairly late in life and became physician to Madame de Pompadour and Louis xv. He started publishing works on economic subjects when he was sixty years of age (notably two articles in the *Encyclopèdie:* 'Fermiers', 'Grains'). In 1758 he wrote his *Tableau économique* (*The Oeconomical Table* London 1766), which outlines physiocratic doctrine. Later on, he brought out a more extensive work entitled *Les maximes générales du gouvernement économique d'un royaume agricole.* Quesnay's chief followers may be said to be Victor Riquetti, Marquis de Mirabeau (1715–89), Pierre Samuel Dupont de Nemours (1739–1817) and Pierre Paul Mercier de la Rivière (1721–93). Anne Robert Turgot (1727–81) took a more independent stand.

Quesnay's underlying principle is that only agriculture should be considered productive since it alone serves to multiply products; industry confines itself to processing and trade to transport. Money is regarded simply as a medium of exchange.

Quesnay divides the active sector of the population into three classes – the producing class (farmers), the unproductive or sterile class (traders, manufacturers) and the proprietary class (land-owners). These he contrasts with the employed, who – still according to Quesnay – form the passive section, which is only of importance from a consumption standpoint.

With the aid of *avances foncières* (investment made by the land-owner to render the soil fit for cultivation, upon which his entitlement, and also that of his successors, to income is based – land development, road-building, enclosure), *avances primitives* (cattle, implements), and *avances annuelles* (seed, fertilizer), the *produit brut* (crop) is created (shown in Figure 1 as having a value of 5 million). Deduction of *nouvelles avances annuelles* (for the following year) and *subsistance* (combined value 2 million – arrow on the left in Figure 1) gives the *produit net*. The bulk of this is paid to the proprietary class (2 million) and the remainder is purchased from the sterile class (1 million). In addition, both classes must buy agricultural products (totalling 3 million), so that the producing class again has 5 million at its disposal and the cycle can restart. Taxes have to be charged solely on agriculture, the only productive activity, and to be paid by the landowners.

In the schematic representation of the system, we see the influence of Quesnay's medical studies, and more particularly of Harvey's theory on the blood circulation.

In order to stimulate agriculture, prices of agrarian products must be freely determined and, for example, any ban on exports is frowned upon. Absolute freedom is the best way to achieve prosperity. Everyone must be able to seek his own interests without hindrance from the government; the individual's interests are at one with society's. Nevertheless, the state must be strong enough to safeguard freedom of action ('legal despotism' theory). If the natural laws cannot exercise their influence free from restrictions, society must be changed in the desired manner (the natural order). Quesnay's disciples were outstanding in their insistence on the idea of the natural order, or the order willed by God.

Appraisal. As the production concept is erroneous – the physiocrats ignore the creative force of industry – the *tableau* too is inaccurate. Yet at that time there was a high regard for the *tableau*; the fact that the physiocrats 'always make their millions work out exactly has a heady effect on them and, like a great many mathematical economists of today, they do not see that in the final analysis all they discover is what they have put in themselves'.(1) Ferdinando Galiani (1728–87) and Etienne Bonnot de Condillac (1714–80), the leading opponents of the physiocratic school, were advocating a more accurate concept of value.

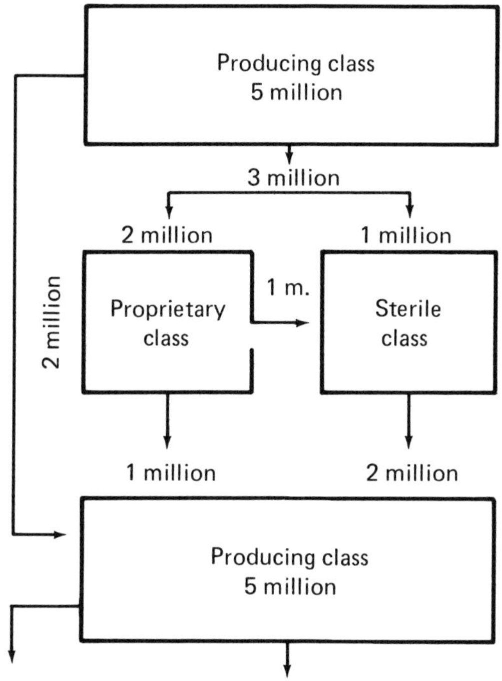

Figure 1. Quesnay's circular flow

The physiocrats were the first to draw attention to the circular flow of goods and money. They also made clear the distribution of income among the various classes.

The physiocrats were the first economic school. Proceeding from specific principles, they developed a coherent theory; in addition, they brought the 'natural laws' concept to the forefront.

4. THE CLASSICAL SCHOOL

The 'classical' authors rejected the idea that manufacturers belonged to the sterile class since industry is as much a productive branch of activity as agriculture. Labour was considered to be the basis of value. The concept of natural order, however, was adopted and developed further. Self-interest, the basis of human action, generates maximum performance (beneficial egoism). Initially, the inductive method was used—starting from the conditions in the United Kingdom at the time—but once the principles had been established the deductive method was followed.

a. Leading Authors

The classical school, also called the liberal or orthodox school, is specifically British. Its chief personalities are Adam Smith, Thomas Malthus and David Ricardo.

A. Smith (1723–90) acquired fame—for a long time he was called the father of economics—with *An Inquiry into the Nature and Causes of the Wealth of Nations,* published in 1776. In this unsystematic and rambling work, he points to the great advantages of division of labour and expounds a theory of value based on labour. Smith is optimistic concerning the effect on output of economic liberalism (but less so as regards distribution). This optimism was not shared by Malthus and Ricardo.

T. Malthus (1766–1834) is known mainly for his theory of population. His *Essay on the Principle of Population* (published anonymously in 1798 and in an improved edition under his own name in 1803) was written as a reaction to the argument propounded in 1793 by William Godwin (1756–1836) that mankind's misery is due to maldistribution of goods. Malthus maintained that pauperism was an inevitable phenomenon, caused by overpopulation.

The population increases, claims Malthus, by geometric progression (doubling in twenty-five years), whereas means of subsistence only increase by arithmetic progression. Malthus is thus opposed to the mercantilists' demographic policy. Unduly rapid growth of the population is what must first be arrested. If positive checks (wars, famines, plagues) do not work, preventive checks (moral restraint) must be applied. This theory, based partly on somewhat exceptional contemporary North American conditions (immigration), had some influence on the public assistance policy of the day. Malthus was very much in favour of the inductive method, in contrast with most classical authors.

Malthus does not agree with J.B. Say's *loi des débouchés* on the impossibility of overproduction (*Principles of Political Economy*, 1820). For this he was later highly praised by J.M. Keynes.

D. Ricardo (1772–1833) goes further in applying Smith's theory of value (*On the Principles of Political Economy and Taxation*, 1817). In particular, he makes a distinction between those goods which can and those which cannot be arbitrarily multiplied. His work makes, however, heavy reading, and is highly abstract and unsystematically constructed.

Ricardo was particularly interested in distribution problems. His views on wage determination ('iron law of wages'), land-rent and international trade (comparative cost) commanded a great deal of influence.

Ricardo also formulated an early but naive purchasing-power-parity theory. In addition, he was an advocate of the currency principle (*The High Price of Bullion*, 1810).

Various authors developed the classical doctrine – in France, Jean-Baptiste Say (1768–1832) and Frédéric Bastiat (1801–50), and in the United Kingdom, Nassau William Senior (1790–1864), who is famous for his abstinence theory of interest, and John Stuart Mill (1806–73).

Appraisal. The classical doctrine proceeds deductively. The laws derived from the egoistic behaviour of the *homo œconomicus* remain as the foundation of modern economic theory. Natural order has developed into a leading concept in present-day theory. Although many theories of the liberal school are outmoded and inaccurate (the theory of value is incorrect, among other things), they are still considered 'classical' because of the way in which they were treated. The method of analysis employed – the mechanism of supply and demand – was later used as a model.

Under the influence of the classical authors, economics developed as an independent science.

b. Reactions

Criticism of the classical doctrine was soon forthcoming from various quarters.

1. According to Jean Charles de Sismondi (1773–1842), mechanization is the scourge of the working class. His criticism of the capitalist system made him a forerunner of socialism; his call for a return to a corporative society brought him closer to the romantic movement, which did not accept human egoism as a basis for economic science. The most prominent representatives of this movement were German Catholic authors (notably Adam Heinrich Müller, 1779–1829).

2. The adherents of the protectionist movement denied that the benefits of international trade were experienced by all nations. According to Friedrich List (1798–1846), the economic development process went through the following stages: (a) nomadism and (b) sedentariness, the latter being subdivided into the following phases: (i) agriculture; (ii) agriculture and manufacturing (iii) agriculture, manufacturing and trade. The transition from phase (ii) to (iii) occurs when manufacturing (or agriculture) has developed sufficiently to produce at lower costs than those ruling in other countries. As long as this has not been achieved, protectionism is legitimate in order to promote the development of domestic agriculture and manufacturing. In List's view, the United Kingdom and France had already passed this phase, but Germany had not.

In point of fact, these phases are interwoven; trade sometimes exists before manufacturing. Different classifications were drawn up, mostly based on secondary factors.

In the United States, protection found a champion in Henry Charles Carey (1793–1879).

3. The historical school and socialism are enlarged upon in the following two sections.

5. THE HISTORICAL SCHOOL

The historical school contested the universality of economic laws, which are limited by time and space, and endeavoured to establish development laws (Wirtschaftsstufen). It exercised a particularly marked influence in the German-speaking area for about forty years (from 1843, when Roscher's *Grundriss zu Vorlesungen über die Staatswissenschaft nach geschichtlicher Methode* appeared).

The representatives of the historical school, Wilhelm Roscher (1817–94), Bruno Hildebrand (1812–78) and Karl Knies (1821–98), laid the emphasis, unlike Ricardo, for instance, on investigation of the facts. They viewed economic data in the overall context of political and social developments. On the model of F. List, Roscher (natural, labour and capital economies), and Hildebrand (exchange, money and credit economies) drew up development theories. K. Knies refuted these theories: he wanted economics reduced to a science of facts, in which every situation had a character of its own that must be described separately.

Knies was subsequently emulated by the members of what was called the 'young historical school', outstanding in which was Gustav von Schmoller (1838–1917). Among its other leading figures were Georg Knapp (1842–1926) and Karl Bücher (1847–1930).

Several of the young historical school's adherents advocated social reforms (including progressive income taxes, old age pensions and sickness insurance). In 1872 they founded the Verein für Sozialpolitik at Eisenach, which had a considerable influence on social and political developments in Germany (especially the social legislation introduced by Bismarck).

In their attempt to study economic problems in a wide framework, some writers later tended towards the ideas outlined above, notably Werner Sombart (1863–1941) and Max Weber (1864–1920).

Appraisal. The historical school had the merit of calling attention to the way in which economic phenomena are conditioned by history. The vast amount of material that they collected frequently proved unprofitable owing to lack of interpretation. Even so, pioneering work was accomplished in the determination of methods of calculation for macroeconomic data (balance of payments, national income).

6. SOCIALISM

In ancient times and the Middle Ages, we already find socialist arguments advanced, but no socialist doctrine proper. Only after the rise of mechanization and the resultant social abuses did a doctrine develop. In contrast with the liberals, socialists do not believe that individual efforts to secure a higher income bring prosperity to the entire population. What is needed is cooperation, which can only be achieved through fundamental equality of rights and opportunities. In the early stages, opinions differed as to how such equality was to be brought about.

Thus Robert Owen (1771–1858), Charles Fourier (1772–1837) and Louis Blanc (1811–82) hoped to establish the socialist society by setting up small communities in which property rights would be either abolished or severely restricted. Their frequently utopian projects were elaborated on more scientific lines by William Thompson (1785–1833), who together with Robert Owen laid the foundations of the cooperative movement, and Pierre Proudhon (1809–56).

On the other hand, Claude de Rouvroy, comte de Saint-Simon (1760-1825) and his pupils Barthélémy Enfantin (1796–1864), Saint-Amand Bazard (1791-1832) and Auguste Comte (1798–1857) advocated a centralized society in which the most important decisions would be taken under the guidance of men of science.

Louis-Auguste Blanqui (1805–81) must also be classed among the 'interventionists', but, in contrast with earlier authors who supported democratic ideas, he wanted to gain power by means of a *coup d'état* organized by a small group.

Developing the ideas expressed by Saint-Simon, a German landowner, Karl Rodbertus-Jagetzow (1805–75), formulated the first economic theory of socialism. This doctrine only became widely known through the activity of Ferdinand Lassalle (1825–64), also a German, and by the writings of Karl Marx (1818–83), who adopted many of the ideas of Rodbertus as well as those of Smith, Ricardo and William Thompson.

a. Karl Marx

Karl Marx's views are expounded mainly in two works—*The Communist Manifesto* (1848) (London 1948) and *Das Kapital* (the first part of which appeared in 1867, the second and third parts being issued in 1885 and 1894 respectively by his friend Friedrich Engels) in English, *Capital: A Critique of Political Economy* (Chicago 1926).

On the basis of the classical theory of value, Marx demonstrated that profits and interest derived from non-remuneration of part of the work performed. Admittedly, the entrepreneurs pay the workers a daily wage that enables them to provide for their subsistence. The labour needed to produce the requisite goods is relatively modest (e.g. three hours), but in fact the workers do ten hours and more per day. The entrepreneur thus pays a wage that is commensurate with three hours' work, but for which ten hours are available. The difference in value, the 'surplus value', is used largely for the production of new capital goods through which the output per worker rises, production becomes more capital-intensive, unemployment arises (*die industrielle Reservearmee*) and consequently wages fall to the absolute vital minimum. Consumption thus does not expand to the same extent as output, which generates depressions increasing in intensity (*Krisentheorie*).

The smaller entrepreneurs, who do not possess the capital necessary to bring their production machinery into line with technological progress, are eliminated and join the ranks of the proletariat (*Proletarisierungstheorie*). This in turn has a detrimental effect on wages, so that misery becomes more pronounced (*Verelendungstheorie*). The disappearance of the smaller enterprises intensifies the concentration of all capital goods among a handful of capitalists (*Konzentrationstheorie*). Finally, the antithesis between the wealth of a few and the poverty of the vast majority of the population becomes unbearable and triggers off a revolution as the result of an acute economic depression (*Zusammenbruchstheorie*). This produces a classless society in which production is based on the satisfaction of wants and not on the profit motive.

Marx follows Hegelian dialectics. For instance, he says that thesis (the capitalist society, based on private ownership of capital goods) gives rise to antithesis (the proletariat, without the tools necessary for the work). From this contrast emerges synthesis, that is to say, the socialist society, in which the means of production belong to the community.

Marx asserts that the way in which each social class ensures its subsistence influences its views on such subjects as morality, religion and science; in other words, the economic structure determines the accompanying ideas (historical materialism). Each class thus has its own concepts of justice. The collectivist society is necessary, not for reasons of justice, but because capitalism, once it has fulfilled its 'historical' role (namely the accumulation of capital goods), is no longer in a position to ensure man's economic and consequently his cultural progress.

b. Followers

Marx's followers tried to adapt his doctrine to changed circumstances. Karl Kautsky (1854–1938), in *Die Agrarfrage. Eine Übersicht über die Tendenzen der modernen Landwirtschaft und die Agrarpolitik der Sozialdemokratie* (Stuttgart 1899, 2nd ed., 1902), attemps to explain why concentration is a slower process in agriculture than in industry. Rudolf Hilferding (1877–1943), in *Das Finanzkapital. Eine Studie über die jüngste Entwicklung des Kapitalismus* (Vienna 1910; 3rd ed., Berlin 1947), studied the repercussions of trusts and restrictive agreements on the functioning of the capitalist economy. Rosa Luxemburg (1870–1919), in *Die Akkumulation des Kapitals. Ein Beitrag zur ökonomischen Erklärung des Imperialismus* (Berlin 1913; 2nd ed., 1921; trans. as *The Accumulation of Capital,* New York 1964), claims that the capitalist countries can only avoid depressions by exporting part of their production to less-developed countries (by making direct investment in those countries). The employment of cheap labour in these areas creates fresh surplus value.

Lenin (whose real name was Vladimir Ilyitch Ulyanov; 1870–1924) was more a man of action. The regime which he established differed greatly from primitive communism, the chief upholder of which was Etienne Cabet (1788–1856), and which proclaimed that not only capital goods but also consumer goods were common property. In the USSR there is at present no question of communism in the original sense of the word. A collectivist system has been introduced, together with the dictatorship of (or better, over) the proletariat (the socialization process not having been accompanied by political and economic democracy). Such a dictatorship is necessary for a short period – according to Lenin – in order to eradicate the bourgeois mentality.

c. Appraisal

Marx's work is 'an unsuccessful attempt to prove scientifically the inevitable collapse of capitalism in Western Europe'.[2] Marx anticipated important aspects of the development of capitalism (e.g. economic concentration) but was mistaken concerning other fields (e.g. the *Verelendungstheorie*). His explanation of these phenomena is, however, based on a faulty premise (the classical theory of value). Although Marx does not regard the appearance of great thinkers as necessarily being the consequence of a specific economic structure, he nevertheless believes in historical materialism. This is untenable, however, since there is an interrelation between 'being' and 'thinking'. The economy is not invariably the decisive factor: 'Never the sole and primary cause, economics is sometimes decisive: however, nothing guarantees that it will remain decisive even in identical situations'.[3]

Why history is to be considered as class struggle, why a classless society will come into being (and why people will be happier in such a society), is not explained. In this respect, Marxism can be compared with a religion. Nonbelievers are mere 'bourgeois'. There are classes (for which there is no specific definition, even from Marx) within the 'working class' in the Soviet Union, as in the United States; however, in the Soviet Union, the ruling class does not own but control the factors of production. The one elite succeeds the other. Elimination of private property does not in itself create a paradise on earth. This is evident in the Soviet Union, where a dictatorial 'transition period' has already been in progress for more than 60 years and where

> after all attempts at socialist emulation, the leaders . . . have admitted that 'in quiet periods' the mass of workers does not act as militants should, that this elite itself, after the victory, has gradually wearied practising the virtue of asceticism, and that inequality of remuneration has, in a modern economy, remained both indispensable and inevitable. Proletarians are human beings, not angels. The revolutionaries, who start by considering them as angels, end by treating them like animals'.[4]

Neither Marx's work, nor that of his followers contains a great deal about the future organization of the socialist society. The economic theory of socialism was mainly formulated by nonsocialists at a later stage.

Interpretation of Marx's works is not always easy, because various contradictions exist (one reason being the fact that part of his work was published posthumously; e.g. the exchange value is *not* determined by working time in Part Three of *Das Kapital*).

d. Reformists

It was not long before a reformist trend set in, the adherents of which only accepted part of the Marxist doctrine. The leading representative of this school, Eduard Bernstein (1850–1932), in *Die Voraussetzungen des Sozialismus und die Aufgaben der Sozialdemokratie* (Stuttgart 1899, 3rd ed., 1921; English ed. *Evolutionary Socialism: A Critique and Affirmation,* London 1909), criticized several of Marx's principal standpoints (notably the surplus value, concentration and catastrophe theories) and urged development of the socialist movement by means of cooperatives, workers' associations and participation in parliamentary activity (e.g. for the purposes of social legislation).

In the Western European countries, rapid economic progress induced most socialist leaders to adopt reformism.

In the United Kingdom, the need for gradual reforms was advocated by the members of the Fabian Society – Sidney Webb, later Baron Passfield (1859–1947), and his wife Beatrice (1858–1943), Bernard Shaw (1856–1950) and H.G. Wells (1866–1946); their counterparts in France and Belgium were Jean Jaurès (1859–1914) and Emile Vandervelde (1866–1938), respectively. The latter is renowned particularly for his *Le socialisme contre l'état* (1918).

Between the two world wars, attention was devoted, partly as a result of the socialist parties' being concerned in the government of some western countries, to the operation of a planned economy, the nationalisation of the key industries and the application of social-security systems. The planned economy was championed as early as the thirties by a Belgian, Hendrik de Man (1885–1953), who, however, became better known for his psychological and sociological theory of socialism (*Au delà du marxisme,* 1927; *Vermassung und*

Kulturverfall, 1951). Since the Second World War, reformists have pointed out that the revolutions by proletarians lead to dictatorship and to oppression of men. It is not so much the distribution of property between various groupings but, rather, the distribution of power that is important. (In other words, the aim must not be nationalisation but rather economic democracy.) André Philip (b. 1902), who draws copiously upon the ideas of H. de Man, states that:

> Nothing resembles an American top manager more than a Russian director or a high level French technologist . . . modern society is no longer capitalistic, yet at the same time has not inclined towards any form of socialism; there is a shift of power from those who own capital towards those who possess know-how. . . . What divides man from man is not so much the property owned but the power exercised; and true social differentiation, whatever political regime may be in power, is between those who command and those who obey.(5)

And C. Bruclain (pseudonym for a collective authorship) states that '. . . the problem of ownership is now . . . of secondary importance. A dynamic private enterprise can in certain respects, be more 'socialist' than an inefficient public enterprise'.

The efficiency of the Western economic system has to be accorded due weight.

> If it is to avoid becoming inefficient or deviating towards tyranny, *modern socialism* must safeguard human liberties and come to terms with the fact that the masses are not likely to sacrifice the various forms of individual satisfaction which capitalism offers or promises them particularly in *Western Europe.*(6)

7. THE AUSTRIAN SCHOOL AND THE LAUSANNE SCHOOL

a. The Austrian School

The purely descriptive character of the historical school's work and the many weaknesses in the classical doctrine, as demonstrated by the socialist writers and in particular by Marx, created the need for an overhaul of economic theory.

In the van of this movement was Carl Menger (1840–1921), an Austrian. By contrast with the classicists, who regarded supply as the chief aspect of the theory of value, he laid the main stress on demand—human wants—and the use value, which found expression in his marginal utility theory of value (*Grundsätze der Volkswirtschaftslehre,* 1871; English trans. *Problems of Economics: First General Part,* Glencoe, Ill.: The Free Press, 1950).

This theory was almost simultaneously expounded by William Stanley Jevons (1835–82), in his *Theory of Political Economy* (New York: Kelly, 1871), and by Léon Walras (1834–1910), in his *Eléments d'économie politique pure* (1874; a second part being published in 1877; English trans. *Elements of Pure Economics: Or, the Theory of Social Wealth,* London: George Allen Unwin 1954). The underlying ideas had already been advanced (but passed unnoticed) by Jules Dupuit (1804–66) in 1844 (Turin: La Riforma Sociale, *La mesure de l'utilité des travaux publics*) and Hermann Gossen (1810–59) in 1854 (*Entwicklung der Gesetze des menschlichen Verkehrs und der daraus fliessenden Regeln für menschiliches Handeln* Berlin: Preager).

The deductive method found a new champion in Carl Menger (his *Untersuchungen über die Methode der Sozialwissenschaften und der politischen Oekonomie insbesondere* was published in 1883; English translation: *Problems of Economics and Sociology,* Urbana, 1963); he is also known for his celebrated *Methodenstreit* with G. von Schmoller.

Menger deduced the value of capital goods (goods of the second order) from that of the commodities which could be produced with them. Friedrich von Wieser (1851–1926), who succeeded Menger in 1903 at the University of Vienna, developed this theory further. Another prominent representative of the Austrian school, Eugen von Böhm-Bawerk (1851–1914), formulated a theory of interest based on the fact that satisfaction of current wants was rated higher than that of future wants.

In the United States, the marginal utility theory of value was improved (the value of the factors of production is determined by their marginal productivity) and propagated by John Bates Clark (1847–1938).

b. The Lausanne School

Léon Walras is known mainly for his studies of general economic equilibrium and for the way in which he tackles this problem, namely with mathematical aids. He was influenced by Augustin Cournot (1801–77), who had already applied mathematics to economic problems before him. (J. von Thünen was also an adherent of the mathematical method.) Whereas Cournot mainly analysed monopolistic and oligopolistic price setting, Walras concentrated on the analysis of competitive pricing.

From 1870 to 1892 Walras held the chair of economics at the University of Lausanne. He was succeeded by Vilfredo Pareto (1848–1923), who developed Walras's work, notably as regards general equilibrium. On the lines of the British economist Francis Edgeworth (1845–1926), he utilized indifference curves. He formulated what is known as the Pareto theorem. Through Vilfredo Pareto's efforts, Lausanne became the centre of a 'school'. Its influence, however, remained confined mostly to Italy (Enrico Barone, 1859–1924).

Appraisal. The Austrian school imparted a more modern aspect to economics. Marginalism was the keynote of the later theories. Actually, there was no antithesis between the Austrian school and the Lausanne school, the difference being only in the method employed. The Lausanne school's mathematical method was later generally adopted.

8. NEOCLASSICISM AND THE SWEDISH SCHOOL

a. Neoclassicism

Alfred Marshall (1842–1924), Professor at the University of Cambridge, achieved a synthesis between the tenets of the classical and the psychological schools in his well-known *Principles of Economics* (1890). He contributed a great deal to the amplification of the instruments of economic analysis, developing the concepts of 'elasticity' and 'external and internal economies', as well as underlining the distinction between the short and the long term.

Marshall is considered the founder of the neoclassical school, which dominated economic thinking up to 1936 (the date of Keynes's *General Theory*). Among his students was Arthur Pigou (1877–1959), who succeeded him at Cambridge. Sir Dennis Robertson (1890–1963) continued the tradition (Pigou's academic mantle falling upon him). Other neoclassical authors include: Frank William Taussig (1859–1940), Irving Fisher (1867–1947) and Austrian-born Gottfried (von) Haberler (b. 1900).

b. The Swedish School

In Sweden, Knut Wicksell (1851–1926) succeeded in presenting the Austrian school's doctrine mathematically and in integrating the theories on money and general equilibrium. He is the one who brought the 'Swedish school' into being.

Gustav Cassel (1886–1944) linked up with Walras and is known for his purchasing-power-parity theory. His pupil Bertil Ohlin (1899–1979) did pioneering work on the theory of international trade.

Appraisal. The neoclassical school mainly studied price and income determination from a microeconomic standpoint, with the result that no attention was paid to the study of cyclical fluctuations. In this field, the Swedish school achieved progress. Thus for a long time cyclical theory developed separately.

9. INSTITUTIONALISM

Institutionalism is essentially an American school. Its father was Thorstein Veblen (1857-1929), who did not employ the term 'institutionalism' himself, but he pointed out that 'institutions' or 'settled habits of thought common to the generality of men', notably 'usage, customs, canons of conduct, principles of right and propriety' (i.e. not profit seeking alone), determine economic activity. Economic systems change with time; technology constantly forges ahead, while society usually lags behind in adjusting to technological progress. There is, however, a dichotomy between 'industry' (technology) and 'business' (finance). The conflict of interests inevitably leads to a socialist or fascist society, depending on whether it is industry or business which gains the upper hand.

John R.C. Commons (1862–1945), Wesley C. Mitchell (1874–1948) and John M. Clark (b. 1884), the son of John B. Clark nevertheless took the view that in an improved form of capitalism cooperation between the various classes was possible.

Mitchell collected a great deal of data for studying the business cycle, and John M. Clark was quick to demonstrate that the market mechanism was no longer functioning satisfactorily and the American economy was being controlled by a small number of large-scale concerns.

After the Second World War, the institutionalists claimed that a minimum of indicative planning was necessary in the United States. In contrast with T. Veblen, they proceeded along operational lines. Among them are included Clarence E. Ayres (b. 1891), Gardiner C. Means (b. 1896), Gerhard Colm (b. 1897), Allan G. Gruchy (b. 1906) and Ben B. Seligman (b. 1912).

John Kenneth Galbraith (b. 1908) may also be classified as an institutionalist. He is the most known non-Marxist author to expose the failures of traditional theory. His view is that production in itself is no longer *the* central theme; collective wants (e.g. social security, urban planning) are neglected. The market mechanism is, in his opinion, being superseded by the decisions of large enterprises (the 'technostructure'), by which demand is artificially stimulated (*The new industrial state,* Boston: Houghton Mifflin, 1967). The economic power of monopolies is neutralised by the 'countervailing power' of consumers and labour, allied in powerful consumer organisations and trade unions (*American Capitalism. The Concept of Countervailing Power,* Boston: Houghton Mifflin, 1952).

In *Economics and the Public Purpose* (Boston: Houghton Mifflin, 1973), which in a certain sense is a digest of his earlier works, the author also considers the existence of small enterprises, which constitute an important sector of the economy (in the United States, for instance, they account for about one half of national production); he contrasts the overdeveloped 'planning system' of large enterprises with the underdeveloped 'market system' of small enterprises. In his proposals for reform, which are based primarily on more government intervention (e.g. wage and price control in the 'planning system'), Galbraith is vague and far from realistic.

10. THE KEYNESIAN 'REVOLUTION'

The General Theory of Employment, Interest and Money (London: MacMillan, 1936), by J.M. Keynes (1883–1946, from 1942 Lord Keynes of Tilton) brought about an important change in economic theory in several areas. Although no model of clarity – P.A. Samuelson calls it 'a badly written book, poorly organized; . . . arrogant, bad-tempered, polemical, and not overly-generous in its acknowledgements' – it immediately had a marked influence. Samuelson, indeed, concludes the passage in question with the words: 'in short, it is the work of a genius'.[(7)]

Keynes does not agree with Say's law. He underlines the possible drawbacks of excessive saving. This was a point that had been overlooked until this time. Keynes points out that the balance between saving and investment will be effected by way of fluctuations of national income. The long-term reasoning of the classical authors was not accepted by Keynes ('in the long run we are all dead').

Keynes stressed the danger of stagnation in the capitalist countries. He saw two ways of obviating such a situation – increasing consumption by better income distribution, and expanding public works.

A rise in income – through the creation of money or the granting of credit for instance – has varying repercussions on the national income and on the level of prices, depending on the degree of employment. The classical and neoclassical authors (Keynes lumps them together as 'classical') had not made this distinction and regarded the purchasing power of money as being determined by the quantity of money and the velocity of circulation.

Keynes introduced several important concepts, such as the multiplier and the liquidity preference.

Appraisal. Numerous ideas, closely related to the *General Theory,* had been developed earlier, notably by Richard F. Kahn (b. 1905) on the multiplier and Sir Dennis Robertson and K. Wicksell concerning the relation between saving and investment. But Keynes built up a remarkable synthesis which influenced present-day economic theory. As a result of the discussion provoked by the *General Theory,* more importance is now attached to macroeconomics, and economic statistics is flourishing.[8]

Keynes also left his influence on political thought. Although not a socialist himself, he had a considerable influence on the socialist philosophy.

The prescriptions of the Keynesian theory (an increase in national spending and particularly in government spending) have not yielded the expected results after the Second World War and have even caused a deterioration of the economic situation in many countries, such as the United Kingdom (where a budgetary deficit generally gives rise to balance of payments deficits). In addition, according to Keynesian theory the quantity of money has little influence on prices. Hence the opposition to fiscal policy by the monetarists (see below).

11. J.A. SCHUMPETER

Joseph Alois Schumpeter (1883–1950) deserves a place of his own, not only because he cannot be classed in any particular school, but also because of his penetrative thinking and the high level of his published works. He is accorded special mention in this appendix on economic doctrines by virtue of his *History of Economic Analysis.*

Like other well-known North American economists, he is of Austrian origin. From 1932 he was a professor at Harvard University. As far back as 1911 (*Theorie der wirtschaftlichen Entwicklung: Eine Untersuchung über Unternehmergewinn, Kapital, Kredit, Zins und den Kunjunkturzyklus*; English translation: *The Theory of Economic Development: An Inquiry into Profits, Capital, Credit, Interest and the Business Cycle,* Cambridge, Mass: Harvard University Press, 1935), he made a noteworthy attempt to integrate business-cycle theory into the general theory of economic development. This work evolved into his *Business Cycles* (New York: McGraw-Hill, 1939), which deals predominantly with the role of the innovator. According to Schumpeter, cyclical fluctuations arise through the irregularity with which innovations occur and the adjustments which they entail. Depressions are an inevitable consequence of progress.

In 1942, his much-discussed *Capitalism, Socialism and Democracy* (New York: Harper and Brothers) was published. He was unable to complete his most important work, the above-mentioned *History of Economic Analysis* (New York: Harper and Brothers); it was issued in 1954, after being edited by his wife, and is an excellent reference work.

Schumpeter did not make the same impact as Keynes. He did not establish any school. (His business cycle theory is, indeed, open to criticism.) He shows evidence of wide reading and extensive culture. Schumpeter employs both the theoretical and the historical approach, although preferring the latter.

12. NEO-MARXISM

Among Marxist (non-Soviet) authors of the twentieth century, Oskar Lange (1904–1965) (Poland), Michal Kalecki (1899–1970) (Poland), Maurice H. Dobb (b. 1900) (Britain), and Paul Baran (1910–1964) (United States) must be mentioned.

Just as F. von Wieser (1851–1926) had done before him, O. Lange proves the feasibility of market socialism (a combination of planning and market forces): Wages and prices of consumer goods can be determined by the market, while prices of capital goods and rents (land) must be fixed by the government. He points out that economic theory of socialism is only beginning to be formulated[(9)] M. Kalecki had already advanced major Keynesian propositions before the *General Theory* was published (*Selected Essays in the Dynamics of the Capitalist Society*, 1971). In collaboration with P.M. Sweezy (b. 1910), who in 1942 published *The Theory of Capitalist Development*, P. Baran wrote among other works *Monopoly Capital, An essay in the American Economic and Social Order* (1966). This claims that it is not competitive capitalism but 'monopoly capitalism' that must be the basis of analysis. A more pronounced tendency towards chronic depressions was predicted.

In addition, the works of Geörg Lukácz (b. 1885), Herbert Marcuse (1898–1979), Roger Garaudy (b. 1913) and Jürgen Habermas (b. 1929) have attracted attention; they revert to Marx's starting point, which is Hegel. Lukácz does not endorse the concept of historical materialism (there is a relationship between 'being' and 'thinking'). According to Marcuse, Western man is so wrapped up in the existing economic order that he is unable to see the possibilities in any other economic system (being 'unidimensional'). He does not expect much from the activities of those who are not blinkered (students and artists).

The relation between Keynesian and Marxist theories is studied by Joan Robinson (b. 1903) in *The Accumulation of Capital* (1956, 3rd ed. 1969) and by the Japanese Shigeto Tsuru (b. 1917) in his *Essays on Marxian Economics* (London: MacMillan, 1956).

Most authors observe with regret that the workers' standard of living has risen considerably under capitalism and that they accept the actual economic order. They try to make the workers realize that they are suffering from alienation ('alienation' being a word that is used in widely differing senses; e.g. to point out that labour does not bring satisfaction but only fatigue, that people become estranged; today the concept is used in a vague and very broad sense: the harmful repercussions of capitalism on human life). It is noteworthy that Neo-Marxist literature is filled with egalitarian phraseology, yet it also indicates the necessity of a new elite that will decide upon what is good for the masses. It is striking that Neo-Marxist theories are 'qualitatively on a much lower level than Marx's theories'.[10] Even champions of the former consider the economic analysis in Neo-Marxist publications '. . . a little weak'.[11] In most cases, a critical approach is lacking. The capitalist system is responsible for all real and imaginary evils. Thus, the greater prosperity of the West is attributed to colonial exploitation. (There is no attempt to explain what the basis is of Sweden's and Switzerland's standard of living, or why Portugal is not so rich as these two countries). Hence, G.Th.J. Delfgaauw rightly says:

> . . . the attraction exerted by Marxism on some intellectuals in these days is due not to the analytical significance of the system but to revolutionary pathos or to the promise to create a new paradise on earth after the revolution . . .

13. NEOLIBERALISM

The centrally planned economy and socialism were fiercely attacked by Ludwig von Mises (b. 1881; *Die Gemeinwirtschaft,* 1922),

Friedrich August von Hayek (b. 1899; *The Road to Serfdom,* 1944) and Louis Baudin (1887–1964; *L'aube d'un nouveau libéralisme,* 1953). In von Mises' view, it is impossible, if prices cannot develop freely, to adapt production to actual wants. Hayek is also opposed to any intervention in the field of prices, because government measures clog the price mechanism to such an extent that further state intervention becomes necessary in order to restore the balance between quantities supplied and quantities demanded.

More moderate personalities are Walter Eucken (1891–1950), Walter Lippmann (b. 1889; *The Good Society,* 1937) and Wilhelm Röpke (1889–1966; *Civitas humana,* 1944; *Internationale Ordnung,* 1945 and *Jenseits von Angebot und Nachfrage,* 1958). All these authors aim at the institution of a system of ordered competition (*Ordo-Liberalismus* in Germany) that would be largely in line with the classical authors' concept. Thus, W. Röpke makes a distinction between appropriate and inappropriate forms of state intervention. Appropriate measures (e.g. antitrust laws) assist the operation of a free market econony, inappropriate measures disrupt it.

Some liberal authors are so strongly opposed to government intervention that they would even prefer to tolerate the existence of cartels. The normal course for neoliberalism would be to contest the monopoly power of trade unions too, but in reality this is not so often the case (see F.A. von Hayek). The probable assumption is that such proposals would have little chance of success.

Neoliberals, notably the Chicago school (M. Friedman, b. 1912→; H.G. Johnson, 1923–1977) are against the Keynesian proposals which assign a more significant role to fiscal policy. They prefer the instruments of monetary policy (Keynes's theory drew particular attention to the fight against unemployment, whereas since the Second World War, increasing action has had to be taken against inflation) and point to the distinction between money interest and real interest made by Fisher. M. Friedman advocates an automatic annual increase of 4 to 5 per cent (later 2 per cent) in the money supply, in view of his reservations *vis-à-vis* governments which allow the money supply to grow out of all proportion and thus accelerate inflation. He does, however, admit that approximately 50 per cent of variations in economic activity cannot be explained by the money supply. Budgetary policy remains important assuming that governments, in pursuing this policy, do so in complete impartiality and base it on economic considerations. The same applies to monetary policy. Accordingly, central banks may not be subservient to governments, and be in a position of total independence in taking the necessary decisions.

Also well known are the public choice theorists, who stress the importance of careful government spending: K.J. Arrow, *Social Choice and Individual Values* (New York: John Wiley & Sons, 1951); A. Downs, *An Economic Theory of Democracy* (New York: Harper and Brothers, 1957); J.N. Buchanan and G. Tullock, *The calculus of consent. Logical foundations of constitutional democracy* (Ann Arbor: University of Michigan Press, 1962).

Appraisal. Any appraisal of liberalism is difficult, since some 'liberal' points of view do not differ a great deal from those expressed by moderate socialists. The reason for this is that there tends to be a confusion between liberalism as a principle of economic order, and liberalism as a political movement. According to the former, individual interests and competition are the foundation of economic progress, and governments are to interfere as little as possible with economic activity.[(13)] Although it is not restricted to one particular party – some socialists prefer a market economy to a centrally planned economy – 'liberal' political parties are expected to adhere or to apply principles of economic liberalism. This is not, however, invariably the case. As opposition against increasing state intervention grows, especially in Western Europe, liberalism as an economic doctrine experiences a revival.

ENDNOTES

1 INTRODUCTION

(1) M. van Meerhaeghe, De la théorie à la politique économique. La comptabilité nationale, *Industrie. Revue de la Fédération des Industries belges,* April 1950, p. 203.

(2) P. Hennipman, Recente kritiek op de economische wetenschap, *Tijdschrift voor Documentatie en Voorlichting van de Nationale Bank van België,* April 1958, p. 249.

(3) J. Robinson, *Economic heresies. Some old-fashioned questions in economic theory* (New York: Basic Books, 1971); id., The second crisis of economic theory, *The American Economic Review,* May 1972; in this connection see also a comment by P. Hennipman in *De Economist,* no. 2, 1968.

(4) A. Lowe, *On economic knowledge. Towards a science of political economics* (New York: Harper and Row, 1965).

(5) B. Ward, *What's wrong with economics?* (New York: Macmillan, 1972).

(6) S. Schoeffler, *The failures of economics* (Cambridge, Mass.: Harvard University Press, 1955).

(7) T. Malthus, *Definitions in political economy* (London: Murray, 1827), preface.

(8) R. Miry, Vraagtekens en tekortkomingen, *Tijdschrift voor Economie en Sociologie,* Oct. 1937, p. 359.

(9) J.S. Davis, Whither now? in *Economic research and the development of economic science and public policy* (New York: National Bureau of Economic Research, 1946), p. 179.

(10) C.F. Carter, preface in R.E. Emmer, *Economic analysis and scientific philosophy* (London: George Allen and Unwin, 1967), p. 9.

(11) K. Boulding, *Economics as a science* (New York: McGraw-Hill, 1970), p. 97; D. Seers, The limitations of the special case, in *Leading issues in economic development, Studies in international poverty*, ed. G.M. Meier 2d ed. (New York: Oxford University Press, 1970), p. 68; W. Eucken, *Die Grundlagen der National-ökonomie*, 7th ed. (Berlin: J. Springer, 1959), p. 29.

(12) D. Usher, *Rich and poor countries. A study in problems of comparisons of real income* (London: Institute of Economic Affairs, 1966), p. 35. See also I.B. Kravis, A.W. Heston and R. Summers, Real GDP per capita for more than one hundred countries, *The Economic Journal*, June 1978.

(13) F. Schaller, Qu'est-ce que la productivité?, *Rivista Internazionale di Scienze Economiche e Commerciali*, May 1969.

(14) P.A. Sorokin, *Fads and foibles in modern sociology and related sciences* (Chicago: Henry Regnery 1956), p. 3.

(15) R. Brandis, An irreverent glossary, *Journal of Economic Issues*, Sept. 1972, p. 108.

(16) G.S. Stigler, The nature and role of originality in scientific progress, *Economica*, Nov. 1955, p. 302.

(17) L. de Vauvenargues, *Réflexions et maximes*, 2nd ed., (Paris: Croville, 1934), p. 29.

(18) L. von Mises, *Human action. A treatise of economics* (Chicago: William Hodge, 1949), p. 865.

(19) K. Marx, *The poverty of philosophy* 1847 – Eng. ed., (New York: International Publishers, 1963), chap. 2.

(20) G. Myrdal, *The political element in the development of economic theory* (London: Routledge and Kegan Paul, 1955); this book was first published in Swedish (1930) and in German (1933). See its Book Review by F. Machlup in *The American Economic Review*, Dec. 1955. See also G. Myrdal, *Value in social theory. A selection of essays on methodology* (London:Routledge and Kegan Paul, 1958).

(21) F.L. Polak, *Kennen en keuren in de sociale wetenschappen. Een onderzoek naar de afbakening van objectieve en subjectieve oordelen in de economie, tevens een proeve van critiek op de wetenschapsleer van Max Weber* (Leiden: H.E. Stenfert Kroese, 1948).

(22) P. Dieterlen, *L'idéologie économique* (Paris: Cujas, 1964), p. 280.

(23) K. Boulding, op. cit., p. 119.

(24) R. Harrod, Scope and method of economics, *The Economic Journal*, Sept. 1938.

(25) See also B. Ward, op. cit., p. 198.

(26) *Manuel d'économie politique* (Paris: Ed. Sociales, 1965), p. 16 [Eng. ed.: Political economy: A textbook (London: Laurence and Wishart, 1957].

(27) During more than 40 years Benjamin Constant collected 10,000 facts, which were to be embodied in an antireligious work. After having changed his mind on religion, those facts still remained useful: 'They were inversed . . . and plead now in the opposite sense'. Example from C. Colson, *Cours d'économie politique* (Paris: Gauthier-Villars 1924), p. 135, cited by A. Marchal, *Méthode scientifique et science économique* (Paris: M.-Th. Génin, 1955), p. 62.

(28) J.A. Schumpeter, Science and ideology, *The American Economic Review,* March 1949, p. 349.

(29) Thus, a liberal economist usually does not accept that private investments are inadequate, because this assumption could lead to more state intervention.

(30) P. Hennipman, art. cit., p. 252.

(31) K.R. Popper, Die Logik der Sozialwissenschaften, *Kölner Zeitschrift für Soziologie und Sozialpsychologie,* Sept. 1962, p. 242.

(32) P. Hennipman, art. cit., p. 253.

(33) This modern conception is in contrast to the classical conception (the task of economic policy is to raise national output as high as possible) and to the more extensive, normative conception (noneconomic standards must also be complied with). See P. Hennipman, Doeleinden en criteria der economische politiek, in *Theorie van de economische politiek,* ed. J.E. Andriessen and M.A.G. van Meerhaeghe (Leiden: Stenfert Kroese, 1962), p. 66.

(34) M. Weber, *The methodology of the social sciences* (Glencoe, Ill.: The Free Press, 1949). Previously the physiocrats and classic authors assumed a normative point of view.

(35) See, for instance, F.L. Polak, op. cit., p. 267.

(36) A. Smith, *An inquiry into the nature and the causes of the wealth of nations* (London: s.n., 1776).

(37) V. Pareto, *Cours d'économie politique,* pt. 2 (Lausanne: Rouge, 1897).

(38) See J. de V. Graaff, *Theoretical welfare economics* (Cambridge: Cambridge University Press, 1957), pp. 142–52 for a survey of the 17 conditions that have to be fulfilled for the proposition to hold.

(39) A. Downs, *An economic theory of democracy* (New York: Harper and Brothers, 1957).

(40) F.A. Lutz, *Politische Überzeugungen und nationalökonomische Theorie* (Tübingen: J.C.B. Mohr, 1971), p. 50.

(41) F. Hartog, Onthechting, *Economisch-Statistische Berichten,* Dec. 6, 1972, p. 1159.

(42) Ibid., p. 1159.

2 THE THEORY OF THE CONSUMER'S BEHAVIOUR

(1) Transaction costs: costs involved in economic transactions, more particularly those concerning the obtaining of the required information, and the journey to and from the market place.

(2) J. Marchal, Essai de révision de la théorie des prix à la lumière des progrès de la psychologie moderne, *Zeitschrift für Nationalökonomie,* Heft 2, 1949, p. 269.

(3) E. Wagemann, *Berühmte Denkfehler der Nationalökonomie* (Bern: A. Francke, 1951), p. 30.

(4) K. Boulding, op. cit., p. 119.

(5) H. Mayer, Der Erkenntniswert der funktionellen Preistheorie, in *Die Wirtschaftstheorie der Gegenwart,* vol. 2 (Wien: J. Springer, 1932), p. 73.

(6) P. Samuelson, *Foundations of economic analysis* (Cambridge, Mass.: Harvard University Press, 1947); id., Consumption theorems in terms of overcompensation rather than indifference comparisons, *Economica,* Febr. 1953.

(7) E.J. Mishan, Theories of consumer behaviour: a cynical view, *Economica,* Febr. 1961, p. 5.

(8) H. Leibenstein, Bandwagon, snob and Veblen effects in the theory of consumer's demand, *The Quarterly Journal of Economics,* May 1950.

(9) J.S. Duesenberry, Income, saving and the theory of consumer behavior (Cambridge, Mass.: Harvard University Press, 1949).

(10) T. Veblen, *The theory of the leisure class* (New York: Funk and Wagnalls, 1934), Chap. 4.

(11) F. Machlup, Operationalism and pure theory in economics, in *The structure of economic science. Essays on methodology,* ed. S.R. Krupp (Englewood Cliffs, N.J.: Prentice-Hall, 1966), p. 63.

(12) R.E. Emmer, op. cit., p. 98.

(13) J.M. Keynes, *The general theory of employment, interest and money,* (London: MacMillan, 1936), Chap. 8.

(14) J.S. Duesenberry, op. cit., p. 27.

(15) F. Modigliani, Fluctuations in the saving–income ratio: a problem of economic forecasting, in *Studies in income and wealth,* pt. 11 (New York: National Bureau of Economic Research, 1949), p. 385.

(16) M. Friedman, *A theory of the consumption function* (Princeton: Princeton University Press, 1957), p. 20.

(17) A.F. Burns, *Economic research and the Keynesian thinking of our times* (New York: National Bureau of Economic Research, 1946), p. 18.

(18) D. Wood in a Note on new books in *The Economic Journal,* Sept. 1972, p. 1073.

(19) M. Shubik, A curmudgeon's guide to micro-economics, *The Journal of Economic Literature,* June 1970, p. 410.

3 THE THEORY OF PRODUCER'S BEHAVIOUR

(1) J. Robinson, *The economics of imperfect competition,* 2d ed. (London: MacMillan, 1969), p. 330.

(2) M.A.G. van Meerhaeghe, *Lexicon van de economie,* 2d ed. (Leiden: Stenfert Krose, 1979), p. 137.

(3) A.I. Diepenhorst, quoted in H.J. Kruisinga, *Het selecteren van investeringsprojecten. Een bedriffseconomische beschouwing van enige aspecten van het investeringsbeleid* (Leiden: Stenfert Kroese 1957), p. 23.

(4) R.M. Cyert and C.L. Hedrick, Theory of the firms. Past, present and future, an interpretation, *The Journal of Economic Literature,* June 1972, p. 409.

4 THE THEORY OF PRICING

(1) M. Shubik, art. cit.

(2) D.C. Hague, The task of the contemporary theory of pricing, in *Price formation in various countries. Proceedings of a conference held by the International Economic Association,* ed. D.C. Hague (London: MacMillan, 1967), p. 9.

(3) E.H. Chamberlin, On the origin of oligopoly, *The Economic Journal,* June 1957, p. 218.

(4) T. Seitz, *Preisführerschaft im Oligopol* (Köln: Carl Heymans, 1965), p. 241.

(5) B. Fog, *Industrial pricing policies. An analysis of pricing policies of Danish manufacturers* (Amsterdam: North Holland, 1960), pp. 28-35.

(6) W.J. Baumol, *Business behaviour, value and growth* (New York: Macmillan, 1959), p. 49.

(7) Cf. W.G. Lewellin, *The ownership of capital* (New York: Columbia University Press, 1971).

(8) U. Ricci, Pareto e l'economia pura, *Giornale degli Economisti,* Febr. 1924, p. 92.

(9) R. Harrod, *Sociology, morals and mystery* (London: MacMillan, 1971), p. 76.

(10) A. Lowe, op. cit., p. 48.

(11) G. Tarde, *Psychologie économique* (Paris: F. Alcan, 1902), p. 176 et. seq.

(12) J. Robinson, *An essay on Marxian economics* (London: MacMillan, 1947), p. 79.

(13) J. Wemelsfelder, *Onaardige economie* (Amsterdam: de Bussy, 1964), p. 191.

(14) H.H. Liebhafsky, *The nature of price theory* (Homewood Ill.: Dorsey, 1968), p. 7.

(15) A.R. Oxenfeldt, *Industrial pricing and market practices* (Englewood Cliffs, N.J.: Prentice-Hall, 1951), p. 577.

5 THE THEORY OF INCOME DISTRIBUTION

(1) A. Woll, Das Phillips-Theorem. Eine empirische Studie zum Zielkonflikt zwischen Vollbeschäftigung und Preisniveaustabilität in der Bundesrepublik Deutschland 1952–1972, in *Studien zum Inflationsproblem,* ed. T. Pütz (Berlin: Duncker and Humboldt, 1975), p. 140.

(2) M. Friedman, Some comments on the significance of labor unions for economic policy, in *The impact of the union,* ed. D.M. Wright (New York: Arno, 1951), p. 204.

(3) J. Wemelsfelder, op. cit., p. 66.

(4) H. ter Heide, *Verslag buitengewoon congres NVV* (Amsterdam: NVV, Jan. 9, 1971), p. 62.

(5) J. Corina, *Labour market economics. A short survey of recent theory* (London: Heinemann, 1972), p. 64.

(6) A. Ross, Trade union wages policy (Berkeley: University of California Press, 1948), p. 73.

(7) F.H. Hahn, Introduction, in *The theory of interest rates. Proceedings of a conference held by the International Economic Association,* ed. F. H. Hahn and F.P.R. Brechling (London: Macmillan, 1965), p. xii.

(8) R. Turvey, Does the rate of interest rule the roost?, in *The theory of interest rates,* op. cit., p. 171.

(9) G.L.S. Shackle, Recent theories concerning the nature and role of interest, *The Economic Journal,* June 1961, p. 252.

(10) G. Haberler, *Prosperity and depression* (London: George Allen and Unwin 1958), p. 195.

(11) *Capital markets study. General report* (Paris: OECD, 1967), p. 232.

6 THE THEORY OF THE GENERAL LEVEL OF NATIONAL INCOME AND OF PRICES

(1) H. Hegeland, *The multiplier theory* (Lund: C.W.K. Gleerup, 1954), p. 252.

(2) T. Balogh, *Labour and inflation* (London: Fabian Society, Oct. 1970), p. 22.

(3) M^*:money supply; V^*: velocity of circulation of money; P^*: general price level; T^*: quantities traded; p: prices (sequences: $p_1, p_2 \ldots p_n$); q: quantities (sequences: $q_1, q_2 \ldots q_n$).

(4) K. Klappholz and E.J. Mishan, Identities in economic models, *Economica,* May 1962, p. 117.

(5) A.W. Marget, *The theory of prices. A re-examination of the central problems of monetary theory,* part 1 (Englewood Cliffs, N.J.: Prentice Hall, 1938), p. 54.

(6) A. Aftalion, *Monnaie, prix et change,* 3d ed. (Paris: Sirey, 1950), p. 554.

7 THE THEORY OF ECONOMIC GROWTH

(1) J.M. Culbertson, *Economic development: an ecological approach* (New York: Philadelphia Book Co, 1971), p. 294.

(2) R.F. Harrod, *Towards a dynamic economics. Some recent developments of economic theory and their application to policy* (London: MacMillan, 1948); id., *Economic essays* (London: MacMillan, 1952), essay 14; id., Second essay in dynamic theory, *The Economic Journal,* June 1960; id., Are monetary and fiscal policies enough?, *The Economic Journal,* Dec. 1964. His last work, *Economic dynamics* (London: MacMillan, 1973), requires previous reading of his 1948 work. E.D. Domar, *Essays in the theory of economic growth* (New York: Oxford University Press, 1957).

(3) P. Streeten, *The frontiers of development studies* (London: MacMillan, 1972), p. 107.

(4) N. Kaldor, Alternative theories of distribution, *The Review of Economic Studies,* 1956.

(5) J. Robinson, *The accumulation of capital* (London: MacMillan, 1956).

(6) W.W. Rostow, *The stages of economic growth. A non-communist manifesto,* 2d ed. (Cambridge: Cambridge University Press, 1960); id. *Politics and the stages of growth* (Cambridge: Cambridge University Press, 1971).

(7) E.E. Hagen, *The economics of development* (Homewood Ill.: Richard D. Irwin, 1968), p. 32.

(8) G. Ohlin, *Population control and economic development* (Paris: OECD, 1967), p. 131.

(9) A.O. Hirschman, *The strategy of economic development* (New Haven: Yale University Press, 1958), Chap. 3–4.

(10) I. Fisher, *The nature of capital and income* (New York: Augustus Kelley, 1906), p. 53.

(11) A. Marshall, *Principles of economics,* 8th ed. (London: MacMillan, 1920), p. 650.

(12) T.W. Schultz, Education and economic growth, in *Social forces influencing American education,* ed. N.B. Henry (Chicago: University of Chicago Press, 1961).

(13) R. Solow, *Capital theory and the rate of return* (Amsterdam: North Holland, 1963), p. 96.

(14) E.F. Denison, *Why growth rates differ. Postwar experience in nine western countries* (Washington: The Brookings Institution, 1967), Chap. 21.

(15) R. Solow, op. cit., pp. 42–43.

(16) K. Arrow, The economic implications of 'learning by doing', *The Review of Economic Studies,* June 1972.

(17) J.H. Adler, Poverty amidst wealth: trends in the world's economy, *Finance and Development,* no. 4 (1968), p. 32.

(18) B. Higgins, *Economic development. Principles, problems and policies,* rev. ed. (New York: W.W. Norton, 1968), p. 843.

(19) W.W. Rostow, op. cit.

(20) J. Hicks, *Capital and growth* (Oxford: Clarendon Press, 1965), p. v.

8 THE THEORY OF INTERNATIONAL TRADE

(1) G. Haberler, *The theory of international trade* (London: William Hodge, 1936), pp. 175 et seq.

(2) J.S. Mill, *Principles of political economy,* 2d ed. vol. III (London: Longmans, Green, Roader and Dyer, 1869), Chap. 18.

(3) J. Viner, *International economics* (Glencoe Ill.: The Free Press, 1951), p. 16.

(4) J. Viner, op. cit., p. 16; J. Viner explains his point of view in International trade theory and its present-day relevance, in *Foreign agricultural trade. Selected readings,* ed. R.L. Tontz (Ames: The Free Press, 1966); see also J.H. Williams, International trade theory and policy – some current issues, *The American Economic Review,* May 1951, p. 420: 'International trade is so complex, so subject to heterogeneous conditions and to ceaseless changes in conditions, that it seems to me almost . . . naive to speak of *the* theory of international trade . . .'

(5) H. Bockelman. *Zur Kritik der klassischen Tradition in der Aussenhandelstheorie* (Frankfurt/Main: Fritz Knapp, 1958), p. 47.

(6) E.E. Hagen, op. cit., p. 445. See in this connection the 'revealed' comparative advantages of B. Balassa, *Trade liberalization among industrial countries: objectives and alternatives* (New York: McGraw-Hill, 1967), p. 86 et seq.

(7) M. Diab, *The United States capital position and the structure of its foreign trade* (Amsterdam: North Holland, 1956), p. 11.

(8) G. Haberler, *A survey of international trade theory* (Princeton: Princeton University Press, 1951), p. 23.

(9) S. Mookerjee, *Factor endowments and international trade. A statement and appraisal of the Heckscher-Ohlin theory* (Bombay: Asia Publishing House, 1958), p. 95.

(10) H.W. Singer, U.S. foreign investment in underdeveloped areas. The distribution of gains between investing and borrowing countries, *The American Economic Review,* May 1950, p. 478.

(11) G. Myrdal, *An international economy. Problems and prospects* (New York: Harper and Brothers, 1956), p. 231; id., *Rich lands and poor* (New York: Harper and Brothers, 1957).

(12) *Equilibrium and growth in the world economy. Economic essays by Ragnar Nurkse,* ed. G. Haberler and R.M. Stern (Cambridge, Mass.: Harvard University Press, 1961), pp. 242 et seq.

(13) See, e.g., G. Haberler, *International trade and development* (Cairo: National Bank of Egypt, 1959); A.K. Cairncross, Patterns of trade and development, *Kyklos,* Fasc. 4, 1960; id., International trade and economic development, *Economica,* Aug. 1961.

(14) R. Vernon, Foreign-owned enterprises in the developing countries, in *Public policy,* ed. D. Montgomery and A. Smithies (Cambridge, Mass.: Harvard University Press, 1966).

(15) I.B. Kravis, Trade as a handmaiden of growth: similarities between the nineteenth and twentieth centuries, *The Economic Journal,* Dec. 1970.

(16) Ibid., p. 870.

(17) *Review of international trade and development 1970, Part I. Recent trends in trade and development. Report by the secretariat of UNCTAD* (Geneva: UNCTAD, Aug. 26, 1970), p. 70.

(18) Ibid., p. 72.

(19) G.M. Meier, *International trade and development* (New York: Harper and Row, 1964), p. 191.

(20) H. Myint, Dualism and the internal integration of the underdeveloped countries, *Banca Nazionale del Lavoro,* June 1970, p. 154. He considers the use of the term 'inward-looking' policies equally paradoxical '. . . when their main underlying emphasis is on economic aid (and trade concessions) to be administered from outside', ibid., p. 153.

(21) M.G. de Vries, Trade and exchange policy and economic development, *Oxford Economic Papers,* March 1966, p. 39.

(22) G. Cassel, The present situation of the foreign exchanges, *The Economic Journal,* March 1966; id., Abnormal deviations in international exchanges, *The Economic Journal,* Sept. 1918; id., *Money and foreign exchange after 1914* (New York: Macmillan, 1923).

(23) J.A. Frenkel, Purchasing-power parity, Doctrinal perspective and evidence from the 1920s, *Journal of International Economics,* May 1978.

(24) H.W.J. Wijnholds, *International trade and payments. An introduction to the theory of international trade, commercial policy and other economic relations* (Pretoria: The Academic Press, s.d.: 1955), p. 14.

9 THE LIMITED PRACTICABILITY OF THE THEORY

(1) D. Villey, Examen de conscience de l'économie politique, *Revue d'Economie Politique,* Nov.-Dec. 1951, p. 851.

(2) W. Sombart, *Nationalökonomie und Soziologie* (Jena: Gustav Fischer, 1930), p. 12.

(3) For instance, in 1878 J.K. Ingram, The present position and prospects of political economy, in *Essays in economic method. Selected papers read to section F of the British Association for the Advancement of Sciences, 1869–1930,* ed. R.L. Smyth (London: G. Duckworth, 1962).

(4) Quoted in A. Gray, Economics: yesterday and tomorrow, *The Economic Journal,* Dec. 1949, p. 517.

(5) Ibid., p. 517.

(6) G.L.S. Shackle, *Uncertainty and other reflections* (Cambridge: Cambridge University Press, 1955), p. 24.

(7) According to E.H. Phelps Brown, The underdevelopment of economics,

The Economic Journal, March 1972, p. 8: 'the study of history forms an essential part of the training of the economist'.

(8) C.P. Kindleberger in an introduction to M. Moret, *L'échange international* (Paris: Marcel Rivière, 1957), pp. 18–19.

(9) K.E. Boulding, *A reconstruction of economics* (New York: John Wiley and Sons, 1950), p. vii.

(10) E. Malinvaud, Positive economics in industrial countries. Paper read at the International Economic Association Conference on 'The relevance of economic theories to present-day society', Warsaw, June 19–24, 1978.

(11) J.K. Galbraith, *A contemporary guide to economics, peace and laughter,* ed. A.D. Williams (London: André Deutsch, 1971), p. 40.

(12) R.M. Cyert and C.L. Hedrick, art. cit., p. 407.

(13) S. Schoeffler, op. cit., p. 81.

(14) A.F. Burns, *The frontiers of economic knowledge* Princeton: Princeton University Press, 1954), p. 8.

(15) H. Albert, Modell-Platonismus. Der neoklassische Stil des ökonomischen Denkens in kritischer Beleuchtung, in *Sozialwissenschaft und Gesellschaftsgestaltung. Festschrift für Gerhard Weiser,* ed. F. Karrenberg and H. Albert (Berlin: Duncker Humboldt 1963).

(16) K.R. Popper, *Logik der Forschung,* 2d ed. (Tübingen: J.C.B. Mohr, 1966). English translation: [The logic of scientific discovery] (New York: Basic Books, 1959).

(17) Example out of A.D. de Groot, *Methodologie. Grondslagen van onderzoek en denken in de gedragswetenschappen,* 7th ed. ('s-Gravenhage: Mouton, 1972), pp. 99–100.

(18) T. Kuhn, *The structure of scientific revolutions* (Chicago: University of Chicago Press, 1962).

(19) F. Machlup, Are the social sciences really inferior? *The Southern Economic Journal,* Jan. 1961, p. 179.

(20) M. Bronfenbrenner, A 'middlebrow' introduction to economic methodology, in *The structure of economic science,* ed. S.R. Krupp (Englewood Cliffs, N.J.: Prentice Hall, 1969), p. 9. See also R.L. Hall, Reflections on the practical application of economics, *The Economic Journal,* Dec. 1959, p. 651.

(21) J. Robinson, *Economics is a serious object* (Cambridge: W. Heffer, 1932), p. 4.

(22) L. Robbins, The economist in the twentieth century, *Economica,* May 1949, p. 97.

(23) *Memorials of Alfred Marshall,* ed. A.C. Pigou. Reprints of economic classics (New York: Kelly and Millman, 1956), p. 427.

(24) F.D. Graham, *Social goals and economic institutions* (Princeton, Princeton University Press, 1949), p. xvii.

(25) R. Harrod, How can economists communicate? *The Observer,* July 24, 1969.

(26) C. Gini, Au sujet de l'utilité et de la limitation de l'emploi du calcul des probabilitiés, *Économie Appliquée,* no. 1, 1957, p. 54.

(27) E. Böhler, *Der Mythus in Wirtschaft und Wissenschaft* (Freiburg: Rombach, 1965), p. 20.

(28) K.E. Boulding, The economics of knowledge and the knowledge of economics, *The American Economic Review*, May 1966, p. 12.

(29) J.C. Odling-Smee, *The Economic Journal*, Sept. 1969, p. 588.

(30) E.J. Mishan, Britain, the economist and the Six, *The Banker's Magazine*, Aug. 1962, p. 94.

(31) S.J. Maisel, The economic and finance literature and decision making, *The Journal of Finance*, May 1974, p. 313.

(32) H.D. Evans, *A general equilibriuum analysis of protection* (Amsterdam: North Holland, 1972), p. x.

(33) M. Friedman, *Essays in positive economics* (Chicago: University of Chicago Press, 1953).

10 THE SIGNIFICANCE OF ECONOMIC THEORY

(1) P. Hennipman, *Recente kritiek . . .*, art. cit., p. 255.

(2) Ibid., p. 256.

(3) M.A.G. van Meerhaeghe, La planification indicative, in *Les Problèmes de la planification*, Colloque de janvier 1962, Université Libre de Bruxelles–Institut de Sociologie (Brussels, 1963), pp. 48–51.

(4) H. Wilhelm, Instrumentale Wirtschaftstheorie und rationale Wirtschaftspolitik, *Zeitschrift für die Gesamte Staatswissenschaft*, Heft 3, 1967, p. 547.

(5) See in this connection J. Goudriaan, *Economie in zestien bladzijden of inleiding tot de analytische economie* (Amsterdam: de Bussy, 1952).

(6) O. Eckstein, *Business Week*, June 29, 1974, p. 53.

(7) D.B.J. Schouten, *Dynamische macro-economie*, pt. 1, *Conjunctuurtheorie*, (Leiden: Stenfert Kroese, 1967), p. 168.

(8) S. Schoeffler, op. cit., p. 41.

(9) M. Friedman, op. cit., pp. 8–9.

(10) Ibid., p. 15.

(11) J. Melitz, Friedman and Machlup on the significance of testing economic assumptions, *Journal of Political Economy*, Feb. 1965, pp. 40–41.

(12) T.C. Koopmans, *Three essays on the state of economic science* (New York: McGraw-Hill, 1957), pp. 137–138.

(13) W. Leontief, Theoretical assumptions and nonobserved facts, *The American Economic Review*, March 1971, p. 5.

(14) G.L.S. Shackle, in a Book Review in *The Economic Journal*, Dec. 1967, p. 859.

(15) H.G. Johnson, The taxonomic approach to economic policy, *The Economic Journal*, Dec. 1951, p. 828.

(16) R. Triffin, *Monopolistic competition and general equilibrium theory* (Cambridge, Mass.: Harvard University Press, 1940), p. 189.

(17) J.M. Keynes, in the introduction to the 'Cambridge Economic Handbooks'.

(18) P. Hennipman, *Recente kritiek . . .*, art. cit., p. 264.

(19) W.I. Greenwald, Common irrelevancies in the contemporary theorizing by economists, *Kyklos,* fasc. 3, 1957, p. 305.

(20) J. Tinbergen, Optimum savings and utility maximization over time, *Econometrica,* April 1960, p. 489.

(21) Quoted by R. Miry, art. cit., p. 359. See also H. Guitton: 'It is necessary to develop economic science which is still in its infancy, far more than to rehabilitate economic policy', (Est-ce nécessaire de réhabiliter l'économie politique?, *Revue d'Économie Politique,* Jan.-Feb. 1975, p. 141).

(22) P. Hennipman, *Recente kritiek . . .*, art. cit., p. 262.

(23) Ibid., p. 264. In this connection, attention should be drawn to the national accounts, which give a clear picture of the main real and financial flows between the various economic units.

APPENDIX: ECONOMIC DOCTRINES

(1) C. Gide and C. Rist, *Histoire des doctrines économiques,* 7th ed. (Paris: Sirecy, 1947), Vol. 1, p. 22.

(2) R. van Doorn, *Uitleiding uit de Marxistische economie* (Leiden: H.E. Stenfert Kroese, 1978), p. 3.

(3) J.P. Haesaert, *Sociologie générale* (Brussels - Paris: Erasme, 1956), p. 359.

(4) R. Aron, *Les désillusions du progrès* (Paris: Calmann-Lévy, 1969), p. 134.

(5) A. Philip, *La gauche. Mythes et réalités* (Paris: Aubier, 1964), p. 188–189.

(6) C. Bruclain, *Le socialisme et l'Europe* (Paris: Editions du Seuil, 1965), p. 50 and p. 57.

(7) P.A. Samuelson, Lord Keynes and the 'General Theory', *Econometrica,* July 1946, p. 190.

(8) In this way, more and more importance was attached to econometric analyses. Among the pioneers in this respect are Ragnar Frisch (1895–1972) and Jan Tinbergen (°1903). Also, many publications were devoted to the general equilibrium theory – by, amongst others, John R. Hicks (°1904), Paul A. Samuelson (°1915) and Kenneth Arrow (°1921). Later, Simon Kuznets (°1901) made an extensive study of the quantitative analysis of macro-economic data (more particularly on economic growth).

(9) O. Lange, *Papers in economics and sociology 1930–1960* (New York: Pergamon Press 1970).

(10) L. Hoffman, Wetenschap of religie?, *Economisch-Statistische Berichten,* 26 April 1972, p. 401.

(11) B. Ward, *What's wrong with economics?* (London: MacMillan, 1972), p. 79.

(12) G.Th.J. Delfgaauw, De economie van Herbert Marcuse en zijn geestesverwanten, in *Schaarste en Welvaart.* Opstellen aangeboden aan Prof. Dr. P. Hennipman ter gelegenheid van zijn vijfentwintigjarig hoogleraarschap aan de universiteit van Amsterdam (Leiden: Stenfert Kroese, 1971), p. 35.

(13) Liberalism may not even be confused with capitalism, i.e. a system under which the means of production are in private ownership and economic activity is conducted in accordance with decisions of various firms based on consumer requirements, since monopolistic situations are capable of impeding the market mechanism.

INDEX

Adler, J. H., 57, 117
Aftalion, A., 50, 116
Albert, H., 71, 120
Andriessen, J. E., 6, 113
Aquinas, T., 84
Aristotle, 84
Aron, R., 97, 122
Arrow, K. J., 57, 105, 109, 117
Ayres, C. E., 103
Balassa, B., 118
Balogh, T., 47, 116
Baran, P., 106
Barone, E., 101
Bastiat, F., 91
Baudin, L., 108
Baumol, W. J., 25, 115
Bazard, S., 94
Bernstein, E., 98
Bismarck, 37, 93
Blanc, L., 34
Blanqui, L. A., 94
Bockelmann, H., 60, 118
Bodin, J. A., 86
Böhler, E., 74, 121
Bonnot de Condillac, E., 88
Boulding, K. E., 2, 5, 11, 70, 74, 112, 114, 120, 121
Brandis, R., 4, 112
Brechling, F. P. R., 116
Bronfenbrenner, M., 73, 120
Bruclain, C., 99, 122
Buchanan, J. N., 109
Bücher, K., 93
Burns, A. F., 15, 71, 114, 120
Cabet, E., 96
Cairncross, A. K., 118
Cantillon, R., 86
Carey, H. C., 92
Carter, C. F., 2, 112
Cassel, G., 64, 102, 119
Chamberlin, E. H., 25, 115
Child, J., 86
Clark, J. B., 100, 103
Clark, J. M., 103
Colbert, J. B., 86
Colm, G., 103
Colson, C., 5, 113
Commons, J. R. C., 103
Comte, A., 94
Corina, J., 37, 116
Cournot, A., 101
Culbertson, J. M., 51, 117
Cyert, R. M., 22, 71, 115, 120
Davis, J. S., 2, 112

de Groot, A. D., 72, 120, 123
Delfgaauw, G. T. J., 107, 123
de V. Graaff, J., 6, 113
de Man, H., 98, 99
de Montchrétien, A., 86
Denison, E. F., 56, 117
de Sismondi, J. C., 92
de Vauvenargues, L., 112
de Vries, M. G., 64, 119
Diab, M., 62, 118
Diepenhorst, A. I., 22, 115
Dieterlen, P., 5, 112
Dobb, M. H., 106
Domar, E. D., 51, 52, 53, 117
Downs, A., 7, 109, 113
Duesenberry, J. S., 12, 14, 114
Dupont de Nemours, P. S., 87
Dupuit, J., 100
Eckstein, O., 79, 121
Edgeworth, F., 101
Emmer, R. E., 14, 112, 114
Enfantin, B., 94
Engels, F., 94
Eucken, W., 3, 108, 112
Evans, H. D., 75, 121
Fisher, I., 55, 102, 105, 108, 117
Fog, B., 25, 115
Fourier, C., 94
Frenkel, J. A., 65, 119
Friedman, M., 14, 35, 75, 80, 108, 114, 116, 121
Frisch, R., 105, 122
Galbraith, J. K., 71, 103, 104, 120
Galiani, F., 88
Garaudy, R., 106
Gide, C., 88, 122
Gini, C., 73, 120
Godwin, W., 90
Gossen, H., 100
Goudriaan, J., 79, 121
Graham, F. D., 73, 120
Gray, A., 70, 119
Greenwald, W. I., 81, 122
Gruchy, A. G., 103
Guitton, H., 122
Haberler, G., 40, 60, 62, 63, 102, 116, 118
Habermas, J., 106
Haesaert, J. P., 97, 122
Hagen, E. E., 53, 60, 117, 118
Hague, D. C., 25, 115
Hahn, F. H., 39, 116
Hall, R. L., 120
Harrod, R. F., 5, 30, 51, 52, 53, 73, 112, 115, 117, 120
Hartog, F., 7, 113
Heckscher, E., 59, 61, 62, 66, 67
Hedrick, C. L., 22, 71, 115, 120
Hegel, F., 106
Hegeland, H., 45, 116
Hennipman, P., 1, 5, 6, 77, 78, 81, 82, 111, 113, 121, 122, 123
Heston, A. W., 112
Hicks, J. R., 58, 105, 117, 122
Higgings, B., 57, 117
Hildebrand, B., 93
Hilferding, R., 96
Hirschman, A. O., 55, 117
Hoffman, L., 107, 122
Ingram, J. K., 119
Jaurès, J., 98
Jevons, W. S., 100
Johnson, H. G., 80, 108, 121
Kahn, R. F., 104
Kaldor, N., 52, 117
Kalecki, M., 106
Karrenberg, F., 120
Kautsky, K., 99
Keynes, J. M., 14, 69, 81, 85, 91, 101, 104, 105, 106, 108, 114, 122
Kindleberger, C. P., 70, 120
King, G., 86
Klappholz, K., 48, 116
Knapp, G., 93
Knies, K., 93
Koopmans, T. C., 80, 121
Kravis, I. B., 63, 112, 119
Kruisinga, H. J., 115
Krupp, S. R., 114, 120
Kuhn, T., 72, 120
Kuznets, S., 105, 122
Lange, O., 106, 122
Lassalle, F., 94
Law, J., 86
Leibenstein, H., 12, 114
Lenin, V., 96
Leontief, W., 80, 121
Lewellin, W. G., 26, 115
Liebhafsky, H. H., 30, 115
Lippmann, W., 108
List, F., 92, 93
Lowe, A., 1, 30, 111, 115
Lukàcz, G., 106
Lutz, F. A., 7, 113
Luxemburg, R., 96
Machlup, F., 13, 72, 112, 114, 120
Maizel, S. J., 75, 121
Malinvaud, E., 70, 120
Malthus, T., 2, 90, 111
Marchal, A., 5, 113
Marchal, J., 10, 114
Marcuse, H., 106, 107
Marget, A. W., 50, 116
Marshall, A., 55, 62, 73, 101, 117
Marx, K., 5, 94, 95, 96, 97, 98, 99, 106, 112
Mayer, H., 11, 114
Means, G. C., 103
Meier, G. M., 64, 119
Melitz, J., 80, 121
Menger, C., 99, 100
Mercier de la Rivière, P. P., 87
Mill, J. S., 60, 62, 91, 118
Mirabeau, V. Riquetti, de, 87

Miry, R., 2, 111, 122
Mishan, E. J., 12, 74, 114, 116, 121
Mitchell, W. C., 103
Modigliani, F., 14, 114
Montgomery, D., 118
Mookerjee, S., 62, 118
Moret, M., 120
Müller, A. H., 92
Mun, T., 86
Myint, H., 119
Myrdal, G., 5, 63, 64, 112, 118
Nurkse, R., 63
Odling-Smee, J. C., 74, 121
Ohlin, B., 59, 61, 62, 66, 67, 102
Ohlin, G., 54, 117
Oresme, N., 84
Owen, R., 94
Oxenfeldt, A. R., 30, 115
Pareto, V., 6, 7, 101, 113
Petty, W., 86
Phelps Brown, E. H., 70, 119
Philip, A., 99, 122
Pigou, A. C., 101, 102, 120
Plato, 84
Polak, F. L., 5, 6, 72, 112, 113
Popper, K. R., 5, 6, 72, 113, 120
Proudhon, P., 94
Pütz, T., 116
Quesnay, F., 87
Ricardo, D., 90, 91, 93, 94
Ricci, U., 29, 115
Rist, C., 88, 122
Robbins, L., 73, 120
Robertson, D., 102, 104
Robinson, J., 1, 18, 30, 52, 73, 107, 111, 114, 115, 117, 120
Rodbertus-Jagetzow, K., 94
Röpcke, W., 108
Roscher, W., 92, 93
Ross, A., 38, 116
Rostow, W. W., 51, 53, 58, 117
Saint-Simon, C. de Rouvroy, de, 94
Samuelson, P. A., 12, 104, 105, 114, 122
Say, J. B., 90, 104
Schaller, F., 3, 112
Schoeffler, S., 1, 71, 79, 111, 120, 121
Schouten, D. B. J., 79, 121
Schultz, T. W., 55, 56, 117
Schumpeter, J. A., 5, 105, 106, 113
Seers, D., 2, 112
Seitz, T., 25, 115
Seligman, B., 103
Shackle, G. L. S., 40, 70, 80, 116, 119, 121
Shaw, B., 98
Shubik, M., 15, 25, 114, 115
Simiand, F., 82
Singer, H. W., 63, 118
Smith, A., 6, 85, 90, 91, 94, 113
Smithies, A., 118
Smyth, R. L., 119
Solow, R., 56, 57, 117
Sombart, W., 69, 93, 119
Sorokin, P. A., 4, 112
Stern, R. M., 118
Stigler, G. J., 4, 112
Streeten, P., 52, 117
Summers, R., 112
Sweezy, P. M., 106
Tarde, G., 30, 115
Taussig, F. W., 102
ter Heide, H., 37, 116
Thompson, W., 94
Tinbergen, J., 82, 105, 122
Tontz, R. L., 118
Triffin, R., 80, 121
Tsuru, S., 107
Tullock, G., 109
Turgot, A. R., 87
Turvey, R., 40, 116
Usher, D., 3, 112
Vandervelde, E., 98
van Doorn, R., 96, 122
van Meerhaeghe, M. A. G., 1, 6, 18, 78, 111, 113, 115, 121
Vauvenargues, L., 4
Veblen, T., 12, 102, 103, 114
Vernon, R., 63, 118
Villey, D., 69, 119
Viner, J., 60, 62, 118
von Böhm-Bawerk, E., 100
von Hayek, F. A., 108
von Mises, L., 5, 107, 108, 112
von Schmoller, G., 93, 100
von Thünen, J., 101
von Wieser, F., 100, 106
Wagemann, E., 10, 114
Walras, L., 100, 101, 102
Ward, B., 1, 5, 107, 111, 112, 123
Webb, B., 98
Webb, S., 98
Weber, M., 6, 93, 113
Wells, H. G., 98
Wemelsfelder, J., 30, 35, 115, 116
Wicksell, K., 102, 104
Wijnholds, H. W. J., 66, 119
Wilhelm, H., 79, 121
William Senior, N., 91
Williams, A. D., 120
Williams, J. H., 118
Woll, A., 35, 116
Wood, D., 15, 114
Wright, D. M., 116